McGraw-Hill Books by Robert Irwin

How to Find and Manage Profitable Properties

Real Estate Investment Opportunities After Tax Reform

Robert Irwin

McGraw-Hill Book Company

New York   St. Louis   San Francisco   Auckland
Bogotá   Hamburg   London   Madrid   Mexico
Milan   Montreal   New Delhi   Panama
Paris   São Paulo   Singapore
Sydney   Tokyo   Toronto

LIBRARY OF CONGRESS
Library of Congress Cataloging-in-Publication Data

Irwin, Robert, date.
    How to find and manage profitable properties : real estate
investment opportunities after tax reform / Robert Irwin.
        p.   cm.
    Includes index.
    ISBN 0-07-032130-2
    1. Real estate investment—United States. 2. Real estate
investment—Taxation—United States. I. Title.
HD255.I78 1988
332.63'24—dc19   87-27207
                                                            CIP

1234567890 DOC/DOC 89210987

ISBN 0-07-032130-2

The editors for this book were Martha Jewett and Marlene
Hamerling, the designer was Naomi Auerbach, and the production
supervisor was Dianne Walber. This book was set in Baskerville. It
was composed by the McGraw-Hill Book Company Professional
and Reference Division composition unit. Printed and bound by
R. R. Donnelley and Sons Company.

Contents

Appendix A Property Evaluation Sheets   **163**

About the Author

Robert Irwin is one of the best-known authors in real estate. He has been a California real estate broker for over twenty years, acting as a consultant to other brokers, lenders, and investors. He has written and edited nearly a dozen books on real estate, including *The McGraw-Hill Real Estate Handbook, Handbook of Property Management,* and *How to Find Hidden Real Estate Bargains.*

Preface

In the past, people invested in real estate of all types in large part as a tax shelter. The value of writing off real estate losses (losses which often occurred only on paper) was a frequent inducement for investors. Whether it was an apartment complex or a small condo, the argument made was: "Don't think of it as a real estate investment. Think of it as a *tax shelter!*"

However, another problem soon evolved—instead of looking at property for its economic value, most investors began looking at it *strictly* for the amount of tax shelter it provided. As a result, many bought properties of increasingly poor quality and found that they were taking money out of pocket each month just to support their properties. However, as long as the tax advantages of real estate existed, that *negative cashflow* could be made up by tax savings. As long as there was a tax shelter, even poor properties made money.

Then, in 1986 the Tax Reform Act was passed and everything changed. Real estate tax shelters were severely cut back and capital gains were eliminated. Suddenly, real estate could no longer be thought of as simply a "tax shelter."

Today, the game has changed and real estate is on the same playing field as stocks, commodities, bonds, and other investments: the purchase has to make economic sense. *It has to make a profit*—without regard for any tax savings.

This change has been tough for those investors, both big and small, who have been stuck with money-losing properties and negative cash-flow situations (which the new law may preclude from being offset by tax savings).

However, for shrewd investors this is a time of opportunity and the wise small investors stand to do very well with bargain-priced properties originally purchased as tax shelters.

This book is dedicated to helping investors, particularly small investors, understand how they can find the real opportunities in real estate today. It's designed to show how to make money investing in real estate—in ways that are significantly different from the ways of past.

This book illustrates how big profits in real estate are possible even with the Tax Reform Act. (In fact, profits will probably never be higher.) It goes on to demonstrate that these profits will come about only for those who understand the new rules by which the game is now being played.

This book helps you to understand the Tax Reform Act as it relates to real estate. It presents you with new strategies. It shows you why you need to find positive cashflow properties. It even goes on to show you how to find those houses, condos, and other properties that can make large profits possible.

This book is *not* designed to be an aid in preparing your tax returns. Rather, it is a strategy planner for your financial future. With it, you will find enormous opportunities unfolding in real estate investment, starting with as little as a small house or condo.

Robert Irwin

1
Real Estate Opportunities Created by the New Tax Law

The common perception is that the Tax Reform Act of 1986 kicked real estate in the head. The common wisdom is that real estate is no longer a good investment. "Get out and stay out," is the alarm sounded by a number of financial advisors (including several Wall Street brokerage firms).

The truth is somewhat different. The truth is that, while the rules for investing in real estate have been changed (we'll see what those changes are in the next chapter) and there will be some big losers, there will also be some very big winners. Many players who were investing by the old rules will surely be hurt and will be better off dumping their losing properties; but, for those who quickly learn to play by the new rules, there are going to be unprecedented opportunities.

These opportunities are based on two factors. First, in many areas, there will be real bargains as existing investors bail out of properties they can no longer afford without the tax advantages. Second, there is a coming shortage in residential rentals that could create a boom in housing values reminiscent of the late 1970s.

Overall, for the player who understands the new tax law, who plays by the new rules, and who takes advantage of the surprising opportunities that are just around the bend, the next few years can be amazingly profitable.

In this introduction, we're going to look at those profit possibilities and see where shrewd investors should position themselves in real estate today.

When to Buy

Before looking at the specifics of what is taking place in the real estate market, however, let's consider a piece of common wisdom with which I find great fault. It has to do with deciding *when* to make any investment.

Back in the 1970s when gas prices soared and American auto producers were stuck with fleets of gas-guzzlers, prices for General Motors (and other automakers') stock plunged. At that time, I told myself that these giant companies (including Chrysler, which was really on the rocks) would come back. I just couldn't conceive of them simply going out of business. They would retool, manufacture more efficient cars, and become profitable again. That meant, to my way of thinking, that their then-low stock prices were incredible bargains.

I rushed to a broker and told him I wanted to buy shares of GM and other American automakers' stock.

The broker laughed and said, "Maybe they'll come back and maybe they won't. But in any event, there's plenty of time to worry about them. If their stock does start to go up, why then you can buy it. But," the broker insisted, "don't buy it now, not when it's so distressed. There are plenty of better opportunities in the market."

The broker then proceeded to show me better opportunities. The problem was that, to me, none of the other stocks suggested seemed nearly as *clear* an opportunity as automotive stock. With the automakers, I felt I was looking at the rock-bottom price. There was no question in my mind—until the broker put one there—that these were bargains. However, the other stocks *might* go up—and then again, they *might* go down. It wasn't *clear*. I went away in confusion. I didn't buy those then-depressed auto stocks.

Of course, you know the rest. The automakers adjusted. Chrysler survived and went on to prosper. And all their stocks soared. However, by the time they began to go up, I was involved with other projects. When I finally looked at the stocks again, they were much higher priced than their lows and they didn't seem like such a bargain. Now I wondered,

"Would they go up more? Or would they fall again?" Now the clarity was gone and it was confusing.

Acting on Clarity

Only when the auto stocks had plunged on the heels of oil price increases, only when the stocks were very low priced were they *clearly* a bargain to me. I was sure. There was no mistaking it. I saw an investment opportunity. But, through indecision (and not just a little bad coaching from a stockbroker) I did not take advantage of it.

I've never forgotten that lesson. I've since invested successfully in stocks and commodities as well as real estate. But I've only tried to invest when the opportunity was *clear* to me. I didn't care whether there might be time to wait and invest later on. I didn't care what brokers who were sometimes too close to the market said. I didn't look for marginal profits. What became important to me is that for a brief, precious moment in my own personal history, the clouds parted and I could clearly see how I could make a significant profit.

A Clear Opportunity

The moral of this story has to do with *clarity*. While brokers and others would like us to invest on a continual and regular basis to keep *their* businesses going, it behooves us to invest only when we clearly see opportunity. Such clarity doesn't happen often. But it does happen occasionally. And my advice is, when you see a *clear* opportunity, jump for it. Yes, you may indeed be a few months or even years ahead of time. But at least you won't miss out.

I believe that an opportunity is now clear in certain areas of real estate. It is happening almost entirely because of the tax law changes of 1986. It is available for those with the ability to perceive it. But it won't be around forever. Here's what it is in a nutshell.

Property Dumping

The new tax law eliminates much of the tax shelter previously offered to real estate owners. In the past, it was possible (as we'll see in this book) to operate real estate at a loss and then more than make up for that loss through tax savings. If an investor lost $1000 in real estate, he or she might very well make back $1100 (or more) in tax savings and actually end up with a net gain (in this case, $100). My guess is that since the 1940s, probably 80 to 90 percent of investment real estate in this country has come to be operated on this basis.

With the new tax law, however, it is difficult if not impossible to make up for real estate losses through tax savings. If an investor today loses $1000 a month on a property, chances are that's $1000 a month gone out of pocket. There's no making it up through tax savings.

Needless to say, many investors who up until recently had been merrily going their way, secure in their real estate tax shelters, are suddenly quite concerned. The same property, which in 1986 showed a profit *after* taxes, is likely to show a significant loss from now on because there are little to no tax savings possible.

That means that, in our previous example, the investor who was making $100 a month profit is suddenly losing $1000 a month on the same property! No one likes to lose money each month. Even if the ultimate goal is to sell for a profit years down the road, the monthly losses are intolerable for most of us. Consequently, many investors have begun dumping their real estate.

The First Wave of Dumping

The first wave of dumping occurred in late 1986 when the new tax law took effect. Investors who wanted to take advantage of the favorable capital gains treatment on the sale of real estate dumped their properties before the end of that year (when capital gains treatment was eliminated). These were mostly very large investors who had tax analysts on call to give them prudent advice. These analysts said, "Get out while the getting's good!" and a goodly number did.

However, the vast majority of real estate investors do not have the benefit of sage, professional tax counsel. Most of us, in fact, simply try to keep our ear to the news broadcasts, our eye on the newspapers, glean a bit of information here and there, and then try to figure out how it will affect us personally. I'm talking about owners of one or two investment houses or condos or small apartment buildings. There was very little "panic selling" here at the end of 1986.

In fact, it wasn't until 1987 that these small investors began slowly to see the light, discovering that they could no longer deduct their losses on real estate. The tax shelter they were counting on had been eliminated. (In fact, not until 1988, when taxes are prepared for the 1987 tax year, will a great many small investors finally see the actual effects of the 1986 Tax Reform Act.)

The Second Wave of Dumping

As small investors see that the tax advantages they previously enjoyed (and which, in many cases, made ownership of their investment real estate profitable or even possible) are gone or greatly reduced, they are going to want out; thus joining the ranks of their generally more informed cousins, the large investors. As a consequence, to add to the already increased number of large apartment, office, and commercial buildings, more and more investment houses, condos, and small apartment buildings have been put up for sale in most areas of the country.

There hasn't been a great deal of panic selling—very little "sell at any cost" attitude. But there has been an increasing number of investment properties on the market.

As we all know, when the supply increases, the price goes down—unless the demand can keep up. The supply has definitely increased; but is the demand large enough to absorb the increasing numbers of properties brought onto the market by sellers bailing out of their former tax shelters.

The Wavering Demand

As long as mortgage interest rates are low, chances are that the demand for houses and condos will remain fairly firm. Lower rates mean that more first-time buyers are able to enter the market. They also mean that many renters are able to convert from being tenants to being property owners. Finally, lower rates offer an opportunity for present owners to "move up." Therefore, single-family units used for personal residences have tended to be relatively unaffected by the recent increased supply of rental units.

However, the short-term outlook for apartment buildings of all sizes is not as sanguine. Lower mortgage rates work against apartment buildings. As we've noted, tenants buy their own homes and move out. The available pool of tenants gets smaller, hence it becomes more difficult to rent units—and all at the same time as apartment building owners are trying to dump their properties due to the loss of tax shelter advantages.

Thus, as long as interest rates remain low, we are likely to see at least a fairly firm single-family-house and -condo market in most areas of the country (the oil patch and farm belt states are certainly exceptions); however, there will be an increasingly deteriorating apartment market. As apartment building owners compete for fewer tenants and strive to dump their money-losing buildings, we can expect prices to come down. This is especially true since it is going to be close to impossible to find investors willing to buy apartment buildings that show losses; and, generally, the quickest way to turn a loser into a winner is to lower the price. The same holds true, though to a lesser degree, for office and commercial buildings.

Should interest rates be higher, however, the demand even for houses and condos will waver as fewer buyers are able to qualify for the more expensive financing. This, coupled with the dumping of single-family units by investors anxious to bail out of their losing investment properties, could cause a significant stagnation and even price slide of all residential property in most major U.S. markets.

The Short-Term Outlook

The picture being painted here for real estate is fairly grim. At least for 1987 and part of 1988, it would appear that the real estate market is going to bear out the predictions of some of those Wall Street brokers who say it's dying. If interest rates are low, only single-family housing and condos will thrive. If interest rates are high, all aspects of real estate will greatly suffer.

However, remember the story of GM and the auto stocks? When things look the grimmest, they are also, very often, the *clearest*. What's likely to happen to real estate over the next few years is a price reduction (perhaps a significant one). It may indeed be the worst of times; but for the shrewd investor, it may also be the best of times.

For the first time in many years, bargains in real estate may be plentiful at all levels and in all areas. For the first time in a very, very long time it may be possible to buy property and achieve a positive cashflow (i.e., the property actually shows a monthly profit). For the first time since the early 1970s, there may be real opportunity out there.

The Long-Term Outlook

Like the phoenix rising from its own ashes, by the middle of 1988 or 1989, real estate could start to turn around once again. The probability of this is borne out when we consider the long-term outlook for supply and demand for housing. The population of this country is growing, swelled by immigrants even more so than by new births. In certain areas of the country, particularly on the coasts, there is a veritable population explosion. In addition, the high rate of divorce in this country is creating at an enormous rate two households where there previously was one. All of these new households need to live somewhere; and the result is that we need many, many more residential units each year. Yet, the effect of the new tax law will be to reduce severely the number of residential units—at least at first. To understand why, we must now introduce a new element into the picture: new construction.

A Halt in New Construction

As long as interest rates are low, we can expect new construction of single-family houses and condos to continue at a strong pace. As stated, there are many people who want to own their own homes, either for the first time or as a means of moving up, and builders are anxious to tap this market.

However, the construction of apartment buildings (as well as office and some commercial buildings) is a different issue. During roughly the past two decades, most of these projects were built with a careful eye on their tax shelter advantages. They were built to show a loss, which was more than made up in eventual tax savings. However, with the new tax law virtually eliminating that shelter for most investors, the rationale behind constructing large new buildings quickly evaporates. This, combined with a market surplus of apartment and other large rental buildings caused by owners who want out of losers, creates a situation in which construction, particularly of apartment buildings, can be expected to grind to a halt.

In fact, that's exactly what happened. In many areas of the country, construction of rental units by mid-1987 was down by 80 to 90 percent. In some areas, there was *no* new construction of any kind in this category! Again, it would appear that the doomsayers were right.

The Coming Demand

In every crisis, however, there are the seeds of opportunity. As noted, the increasing number of households have to live somewhere. Many of these people cannot afford to buy their own homes even with low interest rates. They need rentals. But where are they going to find them if construction of new apartment rentals is virtually halted and owners of existing single-family rentals dump their properties, selling to those who can afford to buy their own homes?

As the number of rental units dwindles over the next few years, there is every indication that we are going to enter an era of massive rental housing shortages in this country.

After several years of almost no new construction of apartments, it is virtually inevitable that there simply will not be enough units to go around. Increasing numbers of tenants are going to compete for a limited number of rental units.

The result, of course, will be increased rental rates—and not only for available apartment units, but for available rental houses and condos as well.

Ultimately, anyone who owns any type of rental property should see a significant increase in rental income; and that almost certainly will translate into significant increases in price. (As we'll see in Chapter 10, the value of apartment rental property is directly determined by the rental rates.)

The Opportunity

Thus, those who buy during the short, depressed period in real estate are the ones who should profit most from the boom years that are likely to follow immediately. Those who don't follow the common wisdom which says, "Stay out of real estate because it is down," but instead consider a contrary approach which suggests, "Because it is down, this may be the very best time to buy," stand the best chance of being the winners.

When rental rates do go up, as surely they must if there is virtually no new rental construction for any extended period of time, those who own rental property will make high profits and quickly. (The trick, of course, will be to find property that at least breaks even now and hold it until rental rates in general do rise; but that's what this book will show you how to do.)

The Kinds of Property to Buy

Where are the best opportunities?

For the small investor, the best opportunities, in my opinion, are going to be in single-family housing and in small (under four units) apartment buildings. I don't like condos or larger apartment, office, or commercial buildings.

I'll explain why in greater detail in later chapters, but, for now, here are some general observations:

Condos. Suffice it to say that, while they are usually lower priced and, thus, easier to purchase, I don't think condos will match the general opportunities in the market simply because they never have in the past. Historically, they have always lagged. They are the last to rise when prices go higher and the first to fall when prices go lower.

Apartment Buildings. Buy buildings with fewer than four units. Buildings with more than four units could also do very well, if it weren't for rent control. In many areas of the country, the landlord is restricted to charging below-market rates if more than four units are being rented. (The actual number of units you must own before rent control kicks in is a local matter. You'll need to check the restrictions in your area.) While rent control is self-defeating (in that it almost always discourages new building), it is, nevertheless, a fact. That's why I feel that if you're going to invest in an apartment building, buy a small one.

Office and Commercial Buildings. They are not relevant to the residential housing shortage; hence, the scenario just described probably won't apply. Also, they have generally been overbuilt in many areas of the country on the assumption that the economy will continue to boom. If it does, they may do well; but if it doesn't, there could be a shortage of tenants and these buildings could also flounder. Therefore, unless you specialize in this area, I would suggest staying away.

Single-Family Residences. They are absolutely the best for investment potential, in my opinion. As investors who operated under the old rules take their rental units off the market by selling them (generally to owner occupants), there could be a real shortage and rental rates could skyrocket.

It Won't Last Forever

Of course, once rental rates rise, it will once again be profitable to own apartment buildings and other residential rental property. This type of real estate will start making profits *without* any concern for tax shelter.

When that happens, probably around the beginning of the 1990s (or perhaps sooner), we can expect new construction to once again start up. Eventually, it will start to catch up with demand and we will have come full circle.

Act While the Opportunity Is Clear

In my experience, opportunities in investing are few and far between. While those who sell everything from stocks to gold to pyramid schemes *constantly and regularly* try to get us to invest, really good investment opportunities only pop up now and then.

In my opinion, the window of opportunity may now be open for you in real estate, perhaps in your locale. I suggest that, at the very least, you consider the possibility that now is *clearly* the time to act.

2
What the Tax Law Changes Mean to You

Written in cooperation with Norman H. Lane, J.D.,

John B. Milliken Professor of Tax Law at the University of Southern California; Attorney with Bryan, Kave, McPheeters and McRoberts, Los Angeles, California

It's definitely a whole new ball game in real estate. As stated, because of the tax reform law, many (but not all) of the old tax shelter advantages of the past are gone. Today, attempting to make money in real estate simply through use of a "write-off" is not only foolish, it's one of the surest ways to the poorhouse.

That doesn't mean, however, that it's impossible to get write-offs in real estate, particularly for the small investor who might own one or two rental houses or condos. In fact, for the small investor, it's probably easier to be successful today than ever before. It's still possible to play the game to win; you just have to know the new rules. (As far as the Internal Revenue Service is concerned, ignorance is no excuse!)

This chapter has been prepared to help you understand the changes in the tax law as they affect real estate investing. Keep in mind, however, that it only reflects information available *as of this writing;* subsequent changes or interpretations of the law could significantly affect the following material.

How Did the Old Tax Shelters Work?

As experienced investors know, real estate used to be the great American tax shelter. We could buy a property, rent it out, and then profitably lose money! It was all possible largely because of the way losses could be inflated due to depreciation, then written off against our salary or other earned income.

For example, if we bought a house, we could offset the rent we received during the year with all our actual expenses (including taxes, insurance, interest, maintenance, etc.) as well as *depreciation*. In most cases, this combination resulted in the property showing an "accounting loss" (i.e., actual *out-of-pocket expenses* did not equal a loss; only when depreciation was added did we show a loss). In effect, our "expenses" were usually far higher than our rental income, and this accounting loss was usually fully deductible against almost any other income we had. By reducing our other income, it also lowered the taxes we had to pay; thus, we had a tax shelter. Let's take an example to be sure we're clear about how it used to work:

Typical Real Estate Tax Shelter Prior to 1987

Property: Rental house		
Annual rental income		$10,000
Annual expenses		
Mortgage interest	$ 9,000	
Property taxes	1,500	
Maintenance	1,000	
Other	500	
Depreciation	+4,000	
Total	$16,000	−16,000
Annual loss		$(6,000)

This property lost $6000 during the year. Note, however, that two-thirds of this amount ($4000) was due to depreciation—an accounting entry. The actual out-of-pocket loss to the owner was only $2000.

Total loss	$6000
Accounting loss (depreciation)	−4000
Cash loss	$2000

The owner, however, could write off the full $6000 loss against his or her regular income. In a 50 percent combined federal and state tax bracket, that added up to a positive cashflow of $1000!

Total loss	$ 6000
Tax bracket	×50%
Tax savings	$ 3000
Cash loss	−2000
Positive cashflow	$ 1000

In a 35 percent combined tax bracket, it meant the owner roughly broke even.

Total loss	$ 6000
Tax bracket	×35%
Tax savings	$ 2100
Cash loss	−2000
Positive cashflow	$ 100

Of course, as experienced investors know, there were two problems with this scenario. First, as we paid off the principal of the loan, we had a nondeductible cash outlay that reduced annual cashflow, but could not offset taxes. Second, the paper loss due to depreciation was not a gift, but only a "deferral." The accounting loss was only deferred to some time in the future when we sold the property. Then it would show up as a gain and be taxed. However, prior to 1987, if we had held the property for the "capital gains" period (6 months or 1 year, depending on what the law required at different times), the tax we would pay would be at a vastly reduced rate.

The combination of leverage (loan financing), deferral (tax shelter) and capital gains made it was possible to buy real estate, lose money on paper, show a big write-off (reduction of taxes) on April 15th, and end up with extra money in our pockets (after-tax positive cashflow).

Buying Property for the Tax Shelter

It's important to notice in the previous example that the tax shelter was the only way the owner made a profit or, at least, broke even. Without that tax shelter, the property was a loser to the tune of $2000 cash out of pocket. However, by 1986, buying properties with actual negative cash-flow and then making up for it through the tax shelter had become a standard way of operating.

Things weren't always that way, however. Twenty years ago when I was selling real estate, investors bought strictly for profit. The property then had to show a higher rental income than all combined expenses *before* depreciation. Any tax shelter that was obtained due to depreciation wasn't a necessity; it was a bonus. But that all changed during the 1970s. Property values rose, speculators bought with virtually nothing down, and (as our example indicates) it got to the point where the tax shelter was no longer a bonus, it was a necessity. Most investment properties up until 1987 were sold on the basis that the buyer could only hope to break even (let alone make a profit) provided the tax shelter was there.

Now, however, things are reverting back to the old way of doing business. In a sense, we've gone back 20 years to the way things were before tax shelters became so important. The reason is simply the Tax Reform Act of 1986. Let's now take a look at the changes that it created.

Writing Off Real Estate Losses Against Income

Under the new tax law, we may *not* write off losses in real estate against our other income. (There is an exception for which most small investors qualify, so read on!) This is probably the biggest single change and affects virtually every real estate investor, so be sure you *fully* understand its ramifications. To understand how the law affects investors, we need to know that the Tax Reform Act, in effect, created three separate categories of income. They are:

1. *Active income.* This is any income that we receive as a compensation for our services. Salary, commissions, consulting fees, and so on all are active income. Profits and losses from most businesses (other than ownership of rental real estate) in which we "materially participate" (i.e., take active part) are also in this category.

2. *Passive income and loss.* Generally speaking, passive income is earnings or loss from a business activity in which we don't materially participate. For example, being a limited partner in a real estate venture would be classified as passive income. (Limited partners, by definition, are forbidden from actively participating in the venture.) *Under the law, income (or loss) from renting any real estate is considered passive income.*

3. *Portfolio income.* This is a new term used to describe income from pure investments. It includes earnings from dividends on common or preferred stock, interest, royalties, and any other similar returns on capital that don't require active involvement. *Portfolio income does not include real estate profits and losses.*

For tax purposes, under the new law, renting real estate is virtually always in category 2—passive activities. It doesn't make any difference that we actively fix up the property, find the tenants, determine the lease terms, and so forth. *All real estate rental activities are defined as nonparticipatory, or passive.*

The Effect on Tax Shelters

The new law specifically states that if we have a *passive* investment loss (for us, meaning real estate rental loss) we can only write that loss off against income from another passive investment, until we dispose of our interest in the venture. We cannot write it off against either *active* income (as from salary) or *portfolio* income (as from dividends or interest). This means that:

- We *can* write off a real estate loss on one property against a real estate profit on another property.

- We *cannot* write off a real estate loss against our active income (salary, commission, fees, etc.).

- We *cannot* write off a real estate loss against our portfolio income (stock dividends, interest, etc.).

What it means, for all practical purposes, is that the real estate tax shelter has largely been eliminated. No longer can the investor count on the tax shelter to break even or to show a profit on a piece of property. Neither can he or she apply real estate losses to other forms of income. Real estate as the great American tax shelter is no more, with some very important exceptions.

The Special $25,000 Allowance

There is a significant exception to the new rule that directly affects small investors. The Congress was under great pressure not to do away with tax shelters for the "little guy," the person who bought an extra house or condo as a piece of income property. (This is the person who tends to vote, so members of Congress weren't doing this so much out of altruism as to avoid a taxpayers' revolt that might cost them their own jobs!) So, they provided for a $25,000 allowance under the new law. We may continue to write off up to $25,000 from our real estate investments against our other income just as we did before, *provided* we meet the following criteria:

1. Our gross adjusted income must be less than $100,000. If it is more, we lose $.50 of the allowance for each dollar it exceeds $100,000. In other words, if our income is $100,000 or less, the allowance is worth $25,000 to us. If our income is $125,000, the allowance is worth $12,500 to us. If our income is $150,000 or more, the allowance is not worth anything to us.

Phasing Out $25,000 Allowance as Income Increases

Income	Allowance	Income	Allowance	Income	Allowance
$100,000	$25,000	117,000	16,500	134,000	8,000
101,000	24,500	118,000	16,000	135,000	7,500
102,000	24,000	119,000	15,500	136,000	7,000
103,000	23,500	120,000	15,000	137,000	6,500
104,000	23,000	121,000	14,500	138,000	6,000
105,000	22,500	122,000	14,000	139,000	5,500
106,000	22,000	123,000	13,500	140,000	5,000
107,000	21,500	124,000	13,000	141,000	4,500
108,000	21,000	125,000	12,500	142,000	4,000
109,000	20,500	126,000	12,000	143,000	3,500
110,000	20,000	127,000	11,500	144,000	3,000
111,000	19,500	128,000	11,000	145,000	2,500
112,000	19,000	129,000	10,500	146,000	2,000
113,000	18,500	130,000	10,000	147,000	1,500
114,000	18,000	131,000	9,500	148,000	1,000
115,000	17,500	132,000	9,000	149,000	500
116,000	17,000	133,000	8,500	150,000	0

2. In addition, to qualify for this allowance, we must *actively* participate in the business of renting the property. (If you think there is some confusion here between first defining real estate as a "passive" investment, then giving the allowance only if the owner is an "active" participant, you're right. But since when has the tax system in this country been logical, consistent, or even understandable!)

Active Participation in Renting a Property

If we own a rental house nearby and if we personally handle fix-up and repairs, put an ad in the paper, screen tenants, determine rental rates, and so forth, chances are we do qualify as an active owner and may get the allowance as described.

Using A Property Management Firm

But what if we own property and hire a property management firm to handle it for us? Are we still entitled to the allowance? Doesn't the use of the property management firm put us into the passive category?

It depends on our arrangement with the firm. If they handle all affairs of the property for us, then, undoubtedly, we are a passive owner. However, if they act only under our specific direction, then we may qualify as an active participant in the venture.

Rules To Determine Active Participation

To clarify active versus passive participation, here are some general rules:

1. We must own at least 10 percent of the property.
2. We must personally determine the rental terms (rental rate, term of lease, security deposit, etc.).
3. We must personally approve any new tenant. (This can't be left up to the property management firm.)
4. We must personally approve or sign for any repairs or maintenance work to the property.
5. We must personally approve or sign for any capital improvements to the property.
6. We must actively participate in any similar decisions.

As noted previously, *active* really does mean *active*. Although we don't need to be continuously involved in operating details, we must demonstrate that we are in control—that we are making the decisions.

Both Conditions Must Be Met

Note that to get the full allowance, we must meet *both* criteria. Our income must be sufficiently low (below $100,000) *and* we must actively participate in the rental activity. One without the other simply won't do.

Special Phase-in Rules

Lest these new laws, which severely restrict the tax shelter aspects of real estate, prove overly burdensome for some existing owners, the new law allows for a 5-year phase-in period. During this period, the old rules will apply to a decreasing portion of rental income (or loss) from properties owned on October 22, 1986, as follows:

Year	Percent of passive income
1987	65
1988	40
1989	20
1990	10
1991	0

But it is important to note that the phase-in rules don't apply to the *alternative minimum tax* which some taxpayers have to pay. Under this tax, passive activity losses are disallowed in full, starting in 1987. (The alternative minimum tax is a kind of additional tax paid by those who have "excessive" tax preferences. If you're unfamiliar with it, consult your CPA or attorney for a full explanation.)

Clearing the Confusion

The new rules, though attempting to simplify the system, have actually proven to be very confusing to many investors. Much of that confusion stems from the new definitions. To help clarify things, here are answers to some typical questions:

Does the new law mean I can't deduct interest and taxes on my own residence?
This is perhaps the biggest area of confusion for many people. What we are talking about here is investment or *rental property*. We are *not* talking about a personal residence.

The new tax law specifically grants allowances for a first and second personal residence. We may still deduct mortgage interest and taxes on both these properties from either our active or portfolio income. However, there is a limitation on the interest deduction—the mortgage on which the interest is paid may not generally exceed the price of our home plus improvements. This means that if we later refinance for *more than we originally paid* plus the value of subsequent improvements, we might not be able to deduct the increased amount of interest.

Be sure you understand the difference. A personal residence and a second vacation home are excluded from the new tax shelter rules. Interest and taxes on them are still a write-off. (Generally speaking, depreciation, insurance, and maintenance expenses were not allowed on these properties, and they still are not.)

Can't I call an investment house a second residence and thereby get a write-off?
This is a gray area. If you call an investment property a second home, you will probably be able to deduct mortgage interest and taxes as

noted, but you will still not be able to deduct depreciation (remember, it never was allowed).

In addition, there are some strict rules that the IRS applies to determine whether a property is truly a second residence or is a business activity (an investment property). Generally speaking, if you rent out a house for more than two weeks a year, you risk having it defined as a business activity, in which case you would *not* be able to take the personal residence tax and interest deductions. (You would, however, come under the $25,000 allowance rules if you qualify.)

My income is substantially lower than $100,000. I have a vacation house and I want to classify it as a business activity so I can take advantage of the $25,000 allowance and write off all my expenses, including depreciation. Can I do this?
Possibly. This problem has always been around and the IRS has wrestled with it. The general rule is this: If you don't use the property yourself for vacation purposes for more than two weeks a year, it is considered a business activity and the investment rules apply. If you don't rent it out for more than two weeks a year, it is considered a vacation residence and the residence rules apply.

Anything in between is a gray area, in which your expenses (including depreciation and interest) may be partially allowed. There are specific requirements that must be met which are beyond the scope of this book to explain. Check with your tax attorney or accountant.

Must I supervise the property myself? Can I use a property management firm?
The answer is yes, but you must actively handle the rental activity to qualify for the $25,000 allowance. As previously stated, that includes setting rents; deciding on tenants; handling maintenance, repairs, and improvements; and making all other decisions. This does not mean, however, that you cannot use a property management rental firm. You can. The key element is that you still make all the decisions.

For example, one property management firm handles properties for out-of-state tenants. To comply with the new law, it has made the following changes:

1. The management agreement now specifies that the owner will actively handle rentals and the management firm will function only under the owner's direction.
2. The owner must individually authorize every expenditure made. This includes putting "For Rent" ads in the paper, fixing plumbing, adding a new driveway, and so on. The activity, once directed by the owner, is then carried out by the property management firm. In practice, the property management

firm determines if there's a problem, then calls the owner for a decision. The owner's instructions are then carried out. Emergency repairs are made without consulting the owner; however, expensive maintenance, improvements, or repairs are made only with a written directive from the owner.
3. When renting, the management firm procures tenants, but the owner must be consulted and make the final decision on the tenant. The owner must also set the rental term, rate, and other conditions.

We have two incomes and make about $150,000 a year. Does that mean that we get no allowance?
Probably. But remember, the allowance is calculated on the basis of "adjusted gross income." That is your total income less certain items which may be deducted, such as a Keogh retirement plan contribution, alimony, moving expenses, reimbursed employee business expenses, and penalties on early withdrawal of savings. You *cannot* deduct IRA contributions in computing your adjusted gross income for this purpose (though you can for other purposes). However, you can reduce adjusted gross income by any taxable social security benefits you receive.

Often our adjusted gross income is significantly less than our total income. Be sure you check before you decide you can't qualify.

My spouse and I both own rental real estate, but only she handles the management and operation of the building. Can we both take advantage of the $25,000 loss allowance?
There's good news here. Active participation by either spouse is sufficient to enable both to claim the allowance.

I know I can't write off the rental property loss against my salary or wages, but can't I write it off against interest from money I have in a savings account?
Simply put, the answer is no. Passive-venture losses are not deductible against either active income from a business or job, or against portfolio income, which includes all interest on deposits, as well as stock dividends and other similar income.

I borrowed money to buy a rental building. Is the interest I pay part of my passive-activity loss, or can I write it off against other investment income?
The law is pretty specific here. Interest on funds borrowed for an activity that produces passive income (rather than active income or portfolio income) is treated as part of the overall passive-venture gain or loss.

For example, suppose an investor has, from a passive venture in which he does not actively participate, a $10,000 profit *before* deducting interest on the funds borrowed to acquire it, plus a portfolio income of $20,000. Suppose also that he incurs an interest expense of $15,000 on the loan he took out to invest in the passive activity. Unfortunately, the rule is that this $15,000 interest expense can only be offset against the $10,000 passive-activity income. This results in a net loss of $5000, which can't be offset against the portfolio income, salary, or any other active income. The investor can't offset the $15,000 interest expense against the $20,000 portfolio income first.

One major exception is that, if you borrow money to invest in income property by taking a mortgage on a principal or second residence, your interest expense is subject to the residence rules and is not treated as part of the passive-activity loss.

I don't qualify for the $25,000 allowance. Can I write off any portion of the rental loss in 1987 or 1988?
Yes, you can, if you owned the property before October 22, 1986, the date on which the bill was enacted into law. Remember, the new rules are being phased in gradually through 1991, as previously shown. For properties sold in 1987, 65 percent will be allowed (35 percent disallowed). In 1988, the amount allowed goes down to 40 percent (60 percent disallowed). However, for purposes of the alternative minimum tax, the disallowance goes into effect at once in 1987.

I own and operate a farm. Do these rules apply to me?
No. Interestingly enough, the new tax shelter rules do not apply to farmers who materially participate, substantially on a full-time basis, in the farm operations. Those who own and directly operate productive farms are governed by the old rules.

Capital Gains Changes

In the past, real estate investors relied heavily on the capital gains tax rate. This was a much lower rate than that paid on ordinary income, and it was available to those who had held real estate for a minimum specified period of time (most recently, 1 year).

The new tax law raised the capital gains tax rate for 1987 from a maximum of 20 to 28 percent. Ordinary income for 1987 is taxed at a maximum rate of 38.5 percent. In 1988, the tax rate on ordinary income is scheduled to drop to 28 percent (33 percent for many middle-income people whose income is subject to a 5 percent surcharge). This will do away with the remaining capital gains benefit, at least until the law is changed again. This isn't, however, quite as bad a problem as many suspect it is. Here's why:

Deferral

Under the old law, one of the big tax advantages of real estate was deferral. You'll recall from an earlier example that, when we took depreciation on the property, we showed it as an expense item helping to create a loss.

Depreciation taken, however, lowers the tax base of the property. This is not complicated to understand, but is vital if you hope eventually to make a profit when you sell.

If we take $4000 of depreciation, our tax base on the property is $4000 lower. For example, let's say our property's tax base (cost plus improvements less certain expenses) is $125,000. We take $4000 depreciation in a year. The tax base is now lowered to $121,000.

The following illustrates *lowering our tax base over 1 year:*

Tax base (purchase price + improvements − certain costs)	$125,000
Depreciation	−4,000
New tax base	$121,000

There are important consequences from this for us as investors. Let's say we buy a property for $125,000. For each of 25 years we take $4000 in depreciation. At the end of 25 years, the total depreciation is $100,000 and the tax base has been lowered to $25,000.

The following illustrates *lowering our tax base over 25 years:*

Original tax base	$125,000
Total depreciation ($4000 per year × 25 years)	−100,000
New tax base	$ 25,000

Now we sell the property for exactly what we paid for it, $125,000. How much gain is there on which we have to pay tax? If you answered zero, you're wrong. The amount of gain on which we will have to pay tax is $100,000. (That's not the tax itself, that's the amount that will be taxed.)

Sales price	$125,000
Tax base at time of sale	−25,000
Taxable gain	$100,000

The point of this example is to demonstrate that taking depreciation for the purposes of showing an accounting loss each year does not mean we avoid the tax on the depreciated amount. It only means that we defer paying the tax until a later date. That later date comes about when we finally sell the property. Each dollar we depreciate (assuming we sell for a profit) will come back to us as taxable gain when we sell. We are simply deferring into the future paying the tax on that money; we are not avoiding the tax. The main change that has occurred in this area is the passive-activity loss limitations covered above.

Understanding the Changes in Deferral and Capital Gains

Now that we've covered the basics, where does the capital gains tax rate fit in?

It fits in like this. In the past, when we took depreciation, we were deferring money that we otherwise would have had to pay tax on *at the ordinary income rate,* which was quite high. If we kept the property for the capital gains period (1 year) before we sold, however, when we did sell, that same money was taxable *at the lower capital gains rate.*

In the above example, assuming a constant 35 percent tax bracket, $100,000 of income would result in $35,000 in tax. However, under the old rules, that $100,000 from real estate held for a year would be taxable at the capital gains rate. For a taxpayer in the 50 percent bracket, the tax would come to $20,000—an enormous savings. For a taxpayer in the 35 percent bracket, the tax would be $14,000, also a great savings. (For simplicity we haven't considered the fact that the tax rates were marginal, but the point is the same—the savings would be substantial.) Under the new rules of the Tax Reform Act, capital gains is eliminated for most real estate.

The following illustrates *tax on gains under the old rules:*

Gain	$100,000	$100,000
Taxable portion	×40%	×40%
Taxable gain	$ 40,000	$ 40,000
Tax bracket	×50%	×35%
Tax	$ 20,000	$ 14,000

Deferral may still work, of course, if we qualify for the $25,000 loss allowance, but when we sell, all the gain comes back to us *not* at reduced capital gains rates, but at the full ordinary income rates. If some of our loss was disallowed and we were, thereby, deprived of the benefit of deferral, we could offset the disallowed loss against the gain on the sale.

In the previous example of $100,000 in taxable gain, assuming a new tax rate of 28 percent (in 1988), the actual tax would be $28,000.

The following illustrates *tax on gain under the new rules:*

Gain	$100,000
Tax rate	×28%
Tax	$ 28,000

This is significantly higher for a taxpayer who would previously have been in the 50 percent tax bracket. (It is much higher for taxpayers who were in lower tax brackets!) However, putting it into historical perspective, it is not all that unreasonable. Just a decade ago the effective capital gains rate was 27 percent. The new ordinary income rate is only 1 percent higher. From that viewpoint, the change hasn't been quite so dramatic.

Suspended Loss

There is one hidden gem in the new tax law that has generally been overlooked. Suppose you have a loss on real estate that you can't write off because you don't qualify for the $25,000 allowance. What happens to the loss?

The answer is that it is carried forward *indefinitely*. You can take the loss when you eventually *do* sell the property in a taxable transaction. You don't get the tax break year by year, but you do get it at the end.

Consider how this affects depreciation. Under the existing rules (the new rules don't actually eliminate the older ones, they just add to or change them), if we bought a piece of property for $100,000 and kept it for 20 years, we would be required to depreciate it each year. Under the new rules, we are required to do the same, *even if we can't write off that depreciation.*

The longest term allowed would probably be a 40-year depreciation schedule. So we'll assume that after 20 years we had technically depreciated the property 50 percent. Thus, our tax base was lowered to half of $100,000, or $50,000 (forgetting for the moment that only the building and not the land can be depreciated).

The following illustrates *depreciation over 20 years:*

Purchase price	$100,000
Annual depreciation (40-year term)	2,500
Years	×20
Total depreciation	$ 50,000

During the 20 years, however, we were not able to write off any of that depreciation against either other passive income or our own regular income. Consequently, that depreciation is technically "suspended," or waiting.

Now we sell the property. However, during the 20 years prices have actually fallen, so when we sell we receive only $90,000 for the property. At sales time, we can apply that depreciated "loss" to our gain on the property.

The following illustrates *gain on sale:*

Sales price	$90,000
Tax base (20 years depreciation)	−50,000
Gain on sale	$40,000

The following illustrates *how to apply suspended loss:*

Suspended loss	$50,000
Gain on sale	−40,000
Net loss after gain	$10,000

After we apply the suspended loss to the net gain on sale, we are left with $10,000 extra suspended loss. *In the year of sale,* we can apply this loss to our other income. We must first apply it to any other passive income, or if we have none, we can apply it as a write-off on our ordinary income. In this fashion, suspended losses may ultimately be used as write-offs.

The order in which suspended loss can be applied to income is as follows:

1. The suspended loss must be applied to any gain on the same property (as in the previous example).

2. The suspended loss must be applied to gain or profit from any other passive investment (such as other real estate).

3. If there is no gain from either 1 or 2, then and only then may the suspended loss be applied to ordinary income.

Of course, this assumes that when we sell, we actually sell at a loss. If we have sold the property for more than we paid (i.e., a profit), then the suspended loss would probably have all been used to offset our gain. In other cases, it would depend on how high were the suspended loss and the gain. (Besides depreciation, suspended loss could also come from other sources, such as out-of-pocket loss due to actual expenses, such as interest, taxes, maintenance, etc., exceeding revenues.)

Does the elimination of the capital gains rate mean that I don't take depreciation?

No, it doesn't mean that at all. It just means that you should be aware that some time in the future you're going to pay the full tax on any money you defer through depreciation. Moreover, your tax base will be reduced by the amount of depreciation you could have claimed (using a 40-year life) even if you did not, in fact, claim it.

There still, however, may be strong reasons for wanting to defer the income. For example, you may feel that right now you need the tax savings, whereas you will be better able to handle the taxes sometime down the road.

You can still defer through the use of depreciation, so long as the depreciation and other deductions don't reduce taxable income from the property to below zero (or below minus $25,000, if you qualify for the special rules). It's just not nearly as good a deal as before.

Do I defer even if I don't qualify for the $25,000 allowance mentioned earlier?
Yes and no. You still take depreciation. But without the allowance, you can't immediately write it off against other non-real estate income. However, you can write it off against income on other property, and there may be some advantage here. Also, any losses incurred that are disallowed currently may be claimed as deductions when you terminate your investment in the activity.

If you own separate pieces of property, it seems likely—though not definite at this writing—that each piece of property will be considered a separate activity. Hence, the suspended loss attributable to each property may probably be deducted when you sell the property to which it pertains.

Doesn't the new rule increase taxes on real estate gain so much that it makes it unprofitable to invest in property?
No, but it surely seems that way at first glance. On a $100,000 gain, the tax would be $28,000, or 28 percent. But remember, that represents a gain of $100,000. Somewhere along the line you either made $100,000 profit or didn't pay taxes on $100,000 (deferral) or a combination of the two.

You get to keep $72,000 of the gain. Yes, the taxes are high. But, most people who are making that much profit or deferral find them endurable.

What happens if I take depreciation and show a loss but can't write it off against anything else? What happens to that loss?
It is carried forward indefinitely. Perhaps this year your income is so high that you don't qualify for the allowance. But next year you may have a much lower income. At that time, you might be able to deduct

the full loss you've been carrying forward, depending on how much tax loss the property shows for that year. Also, as mentioned before, when you dispose of your interest in an activity in a taxable transaction, you can write off the suspended loss.

Suppose I give away property which produced losses that I could not take advantage of? Can I claim the losses at the date of gift?
No, because a gift is not a taxable transaction. In this situation, the law provides that your donee increases the tax base of the property by the amount of the suspended losses, but they can't be claimed, as such, by either you or the donee. The law is quite unclear as to what happens after other tax-free dispositions of a passive activity, such as transfers from an individual to a partnership or corporation. You should consult a competent tax attorney or accountant if you have a question in this area.

Suppose I make an installment sale of property on which I had suspended losses. When can I claim them?
Assuming that the sale is treated as a termination of the activity, you can claim the losses in proportion to the gain you recognize on the installment sale, that is, over the term of the note you get. For example, if the note is for 5 years with 20 percent of the gain recognized each year, then 20 percent of the loss could be recognized each year. If you elect to take the gain in the year of sale, you can claim the loss then.

What if I make a sale to my children or siblings? Can I claim the loss in this situation?
Another special rule applies to this case. Sales to close relatives or related entities like family trusts or corporations don't allow immediate deduction of the loss. The loss remains suspended until the related party disposes of the property to an unrelated party. Apparently, your buyer cannot use suspended losses against passive income that is realized in his or her own right. However, *you* can take advantage of the suspended loss to offset future passive income; it stays with you, in this case.

The New Rules on Depreciation

The new tax law lengthened the depreciation term for residential real estate from the previous term of 19 years. Now, depreciation on residential property can only be taken using the straight-line method (i.e., the same amount of depreciation per year over the length of the mortgage) and for a minimum time period of 27½ years. (When calculating the term, all property is presumed to be put into service in the middle of the month.) For nonresidential real estate (office buildings, motels, shopping centers, etc.) the minimum term is 31½ years.

I bought my property back in 1986 and my accountant set me up with a 19-year, straight-line depreciation schedule. Do I now have to change that to a longer term because of the new tax law?
No. The new rules apply only to property placed in service after December 31, 1986. There is even a transition rule regarding property acquired or constructed pursuant to a contract which was binding as of March 1, 1986. If you made such a contract, you have until December 31, 1990 to acquire the property or complete the building and put it into service. If you actually put the building in service by that date, you can use the old 19-year term.

I bought my property several years ago and I am using an accelerated depreciation schedule. Can I continue to use that under the new tax rules?
Yes. As long as it was set up prior to the new tax law taking effect and was allowed in the year it was established, you may continue to use it.

However, under the new law, the accelerated portion of the depreciation remains a tax preference item (as it was under the old law). The excess must be added to taxable income, and many other adjustments made, to determine your alternative minimum taxable income. Under the new law, the tax paid for a year is the higher of the 28 percent rate on regular taxable income (reduced by the full depreciation allowance), or a 21 percent rate on alternative minimum taxable income (reduced only by straight-line depreciation and adjusted in many other ways).

I am using a shorter-term depreciation schedule because I bought my property prior to 1987. But now I want to sell. Can the new owner take over my old depreciation schedule?
No. Each time the property changes hands a totally new depreciation term begins. If you sell now, the new buyer will have to abide by the new, longer-term rules, regardless of what depreciation schedule you currently may be using on your property.

I have an apartment building that I am renting on a short-term basis. Most of my tenants stay less than a month. Do I qualify for the shorter residential depreciation term, or do I have to use the longer, nonresidential term?
You probably would not qualify as a residential building. The income

tax regulations are specific with regard to "transients." These are tenants who rent their units for less than 30 days. If more than half of the units in a building are rented to transients as defined here, the building is commercial rather than residential.

I sold my property several years ago under an installment sale and each year that I've received a payment, I've used the capital gains rate to calculate my tax. Can't I continue to use it in the future because the property was sold before the new tax law took effect?
Sorry. Even if the transaction was closed years ago, taxable gain coming to you after 1987 will be taxed at the same rate as ordinary income. The capital gains rate is gone.

Changes with Regard to Installment Sales

The new tax law can have a significant effect on installment sales. Installment sales are those in which the buyer pays for the property in regular installments over a period of years. (For example, the seller takes back a 5-year note for part of the down payment.)

In the past, qualifying installment payments were treated as capital gains and given the benefit of the lower tax rate. Furthermore, the tax was payable only as collections on the note were made. For example, if the taxpayer's base was $50,000, and he or she sold property for $100,000 cash down and a 5-year note payable at the rate of $80,000 per year plus interest, the total gain was $450,000. In the year of sale, $90,000 of the profit was taxable, and $72,000 more was taxable in each subsequent year, as payments occurred.

Now, payments made under installment sales will be taxed pretty much like ordinary income. Those payments will not have the benefit of the old capital gains tax. Even worse, you will often have to pay the tax on part or all of the profit immediately at the date of sale, rather than over the period of payments.

If you are owed any money at the time you make the sale, some of your profit will be taxed at once, unless the property was your principal residence or the selling price was under $150,000. The details of this rule are very complicated, but the basic idea is to prevent people from deferring their gain while generating cash by borrowing against the note they are owed.

Also, for purposes of the alternative minimum tax, the profit is reportable in the year of sale, again, unless the selling price is less than $150,000 or the property was your principal residence. If you pay the alternative minimum tax as a result of the sale, you can offset the tax attributable to the sale against your regular tax liability in future years, as collections occur. But this is likely to be so complicated to handle that you might be better off just paying the tax up front and not bothering with the installment tax treatment at all.

Changes in the At-Risk Rules

In the past, one of the bigger advantages to sophisticated real estate investors has been the ability to write off losses greater than the amount of money actually put at risk. This has been particularly true in the cases of certain limited partnerships. Here, the investor would sign a note for a substantial amount of money. However, the investor would not guarantee to repay that note (i.e., would not be personally at risk). As a result, the investor often could write off losses in excess of the amount of money he or she actually risked on the deal. An example should help to clarify this:

A limited partnership was set up to purchase an office building. The seller was also the general partner. To induce limited partners to join, the seller required that they each put up $50,000 in cash. He would then take back a note for $450,000 from each partner. The note, however, would be "nonrecourse," i.e., if the project failed, the limited partner would not be liable for repayment.

The limited partner's total investment, therefore, came to $500,000 ($50,000 in cash and a $450,000 nonrecourse note). In many such cases, the project was typically so overleveraged that the tax losses were enormous. Over a period of years, the limited partner might write off $250,000. (In a 50 percent tax bracket that meant a tax savings of $125,000.)

Eventually, because of the overleveraging, the partnership might become insolvent. With the partnership failed, the limited partners would lose their original $50,000, and the owner would take back his property.

From the owner's perspective it was great. He got $50,000 cash up front from each partner and eventually got the property back.

From the investor's standpoint it was equally great for a while. He or she invested $50,000 and, in the 50 percent tax bracket, got a tax savings worth $125,000 in cash.

(Although the return of the property to the seller should have generated a taxable gain, many people "forgot" to report the gain on foreclosure, and they were not always audited. Thus, from the IRS's viewpoint, overleveraging was something less than great.)

Under the new law, such not-at-risk shelters are done away with. Now, any nonrecourse financing that comes from the seller is not treated as at-risk for the buyer. In the above example, the limited partner's investment would only be $50,000, and that's the maximum amount of write-off he or she could get.

I'm buying a rental house and getting a 90 percent mortgage from the seller. Does this mean that I can't write off more than the 10 percent I'm putting down?
You can write off the full amount, *provided* you offer the seller personal liability. If you aren't personally liable, then it's not considered money at risk.

A simple trust deed with the property as sole collateral may not be enough. You may need to have an agreement specifying that, even in a default sale, should the property bring less than the mortgage amount, you will satisfy the deficiency. (This agreement must be enforceable under state law.)

I'm buying a rental condo and getting 90 percent financing through a savings and loan association. Do I have to be personally liable to get a write-off for more than my down payment?
No. Any conventional (third-party) financing is presumed to be at-risk money. Even if there is no personal liability, it will be presumed that you are at risk for the full amount. The goal of the ruling was to stop abusive limited partnership tax shelters. It was not intended to hurt the small investor who is legitimately buying real estate for investment purposes.

Low-Income Housing Rules

Although the new law obviously cracks down hard on most existing tax shelters, it actually creates a small new one for certain people who invest in new or substantially rehabilitated low-income housing. Such projects placed in service in 1987 will qualify investors for a credit of about 9 percent of the cost of construction or rehabilitation (not purchase price of the building being rehabilitated), each year for 10 years. (If financing is federally subsidized or financed with tax-exempt bonds, the credit is only 4 percent per year for 10 years.) To qualify for the credit, however, investors must comply with a vast number of technical rules, including very precise definitions of who can occupy the building.

Also, you must obtain authorization from a state or local housing agency to get the credit, because the amount of credit that may be claimed in each state is limited by an overall ceiling. Moreover, the credit allowed is subject to the passive-loss rules.

Unless you are an active participant in constructing and managing the building, you won't be able to use the credit to offset active income or portfolio income. Each dollar of credit is considered the equivalent of about $3.50 of loss for purposes of the $25,000 allowance to active participants. Thus, it does not seem that many individuals will get benefits from this new allowance. It makes you wonder why Congress enacts a subsidy program and then makes it impossible for most people to get the subsidy.

Strategies for Legally Getting Tax Write-Offs on Property

There are three basic techniques for trying to avoid the passive-activity rules and continue to derive some tax shelter from real estate ownership:

1. Generate passive income (to offset passive losses).

2. Terminate activities to claim suspended losses.

3. Use corporations (other than Subchapter S corporations) to hold real estate. (A Subchapter S corporation is a nonpublic corporation that qualifies for and elects to receive tax treatment similar to a partnership.)

Increasing Passive-Activity Income

In the past, as noted, many people owned real estate that produced huge tax losses, thanks to a combination of depreciation and interest. The new law effectively precludes individuals from doing this. By reducing the amount of leverage in a deal, i.e., by putting up more cash and taking out a smaller loan, some of the benefits of depreciation may still be realized.

Let's look again at our first example:

Typical Real Estate Tax Shelter Prior to 1987

Property: Rental house		
Annual rental income		$10,000
Annual expenses:		
Mortgage interest	$9,000	
Property taxes	1,500	
Maintenance	1,000	
Other	500	

Typical Real Estate Tax Shelter Prior to 1987 (*Continued*)

Property: Rental house		
Depreciation	+4,000	
Total	$16,000	−16,000
Annual Loss		$(6,000)

We can reduce the annual nondeductible loss considerably by putting up more cash and taking out a smaller loan. For example, if we reduce the financing by two-thirds, the interest deduction will shrink from $9000 to $3000, and the property will no longer show a tax loss.

Mortgage interest	$3000
Property taxes	1500
Maintenance	1000
Other	+500
Annual expenses	$6000

Since the annual income on the property is $10,000 and the expenses are only $6000, we actually have available $4000 cash profit against which we can apply the $4000 depreciation and on which we will not have to pay tax.

Many investment houses and promoters are now offering unleveraged or low-leveraged real estate investments, often with little economic risk. Income from these properties is passive income, under the literal text of the law, and it can be offset by tax shelter losses, even though interest and dividend income cannot be. *If you own property that is currently throwing off losses, you may wish to move money out of assets that pay interest and dividends and into these "income shelter" deals.*

Termination of Investments

Passive-activity losses can be used to reduce tax liability on the gain from the sale of that activity, and if the activity is completely terminated, it can even offset active income or portfolio income in that year and thereafter. Although the IRS has not yet announced rules to establish when an activity is deemed completely terminated, it seems likely that it will hold that several different pieces of property are different activities, at least if there is no economic or functional integration among them. So, properly timing sales will probably be a useful technique to unlock these losses.

Remember, the loss you cannot take year by year may be the loss you can take at the time of sale.

Use of Corporations

Many individuals are wondering if they can somehow circumvent the new tax law by placing property they own into a corporation. The idea is that the corporation will be able to deduct losses on the property from its regular business income.

The limits on the use of passive-activity losses and credits against non-passive income, however, *do* apply to small, closely held corporations, as well as to individuals. But there are some important differences.

If the corporation is *not* a Subchapter S corporation, it may use its passive-activity losses to offset active business income, but not to offset its portfolio income from interest dividends or capital gains. [Subchapter S corporations are those whose shareholders can and do elect to treat much like partnerships; the corporations are not separately taxable (with some exceptions), and their income or loss (including passive-activity losses) pass through to shareholders and are taken into account on the shareholders' individual returns.]

For example, if you own all of the stock of a corporation engaged in manufacturing or retail trade, you can have the corporation buy some real property with tax shelter characteristics. The tax loss can be offset against the corporation's profits and eliminate some or all of the corporate tax payable.

However, there is a price to be paid for use of the corporate form in this way: Dividends paid by the corporation will often be taxable to shareholders even when the corporation's own tax returns show a loss or that it is a break-even operation.

Furthermore, if the corporation sells any of its assets, it has to pay tax on the profits and the shareholder has to pay tax on any dividends on the profits. Now, even if the corporation liquidates, there is usually a double tax on its accrued profit: Tax will be imposed on the difference between the value of the property and the corporation's tax base, as well as on the excess of the liquidating distribution (i.e., what is left after paying the corporate tax) over the shareholder's tax base in his or her stock (which is often very low).

Some exceptions to the double tax do apply, especially for corporations in existence before 1987, that liquidate before 1989, for which the stock is worth less than $5 million, and that meet other conditions. Because of the complexity of the rules, you should see a tax attorney or accountant if this exception might apply to you.

Despite these drawbacks, in the future it may still be attractive for corporations to acquire real property, especially if they don't pay much in the way of dividends and don't plan to liquidate for a long time. They can still enjoy much of the benefits of the old tax shelter rules.

A Mixed Bag

What should be clear is that, while the new tax law does indeed significantly change the nature of investing in real estate, it does not kill real estate as a viable investment vehicle. Rather, what's needed now are new strategies for investing. We'll go into these in the next chapter.

3

New Strategies for Profits

How do you take advantage of the new real estate investment opportunities brought about by the tax law change? How have the changes necessitated a new investing perspective? How do they affect your personal investment strategy?

Real estate investing has undergone a structural alteration because of the tax reform law. The strategies that have proved successful for the past several decades may no longer be workable. For the wise investor (large or small), it's time to rethink first, whether it makes sense to invest in real estate at all and, second, if it does, how should such an investment be structured today. In this chapter, we will look at new strategies for making profits in real estate, as well as examine some pitfalls to avoid.

In the last chapter, we saw that the two biggest changes in the tax law were the severe reduction of tax shelters and the elimination of capital gains. These two alone are producing the biggest effects on real estate investing.

Eventual Elimination of All Tax Shelter?

As we've seen, the ability to write off real estate losses has been severely cut. The maximum allowance today is $25,000, and that applies only if our gross adjusted income is under $100,000 (to get the full allowance).

While this means that the write-off is still available for many investors, it doesn't guarantee it's always going to be there. It's important to understand that this reduction in tax shelter is only the latest step in a long history of reductions.

Congress has been working for over 20 years to reduce real estate tax advantages. Mature investors will recall a time when prepaid interest, for example, was fully deductible or when accelerated depreciation was the norm. These were reduced piecemeal by previous tax revision laws, and the most recent tax shelter cuts to real estate can only be seen as just another step in the same direction. In other words, what we are witnessing is a long-term process, the ultimate goal of which is to eliminate any and all tax advantages from owning real property.

Thus, while many readers find they may still qualify for a real estate write-off today, it's not the time for rejoicing. The executioner's axe has only been delayed, not stayed. The current $25,000 tax advantage could be taken away by Congress at any time.

Additionally, it's ironic that, as we become more successful and our incomes go up (particularly in two-income families), we also price ourselves out of the $25,000 allowance, even under the current rules.

All of which is to say that a wise strategy for today is to purchase real estate without counting on any write-off. That way if we get it, it's a bonus. If we don't, we aren't in trouble.

The Impact of No Capital Gains

The second big change in the law does away with capital gains. You'll recall that one of the big advantages to real estate as an investment was that we could defer income to the future when we would pay a vastly reduced capital gains tax rate on it.

This advantage has been stripped away. Now, even if we defer to the future, we still end up paying ordinary income tax rates.

All of which is to say that today, even if we could show an accounting loss on property, we might not want to. Those of us who do qualify under the $25,000 may want to reconsider. Yes, we may be able to defer some income into the future. However, if we do, instead of paying each year on a relatively small amount, we'll end up paying the same tax rate on a large amount when we sell.

Buying for Profit Only

The true impact of the elimination of capital gains and the reduction of the tax shelter on real estate is that it no longer really makes sense to buy a property that loses money. While at first glance this may seem simple-minded, a moment's consideration will reveal that it turns the whole real estate market topsy-turvy.

Living in the Past with Negative Cashflow

In the past, when real estate tax shelters were readily available, buying properties that annually lost money was not only feasible, it made good sense. In those days, what we lost out of pocket, we often could make back and more out of tax savings on April 15th.

In fact, experienced investors did not think in terms of losing money out of their pockets. Rather, the term "negative cashflow" was popularly used. As those who've invested know, this simply meant that each month you would take money out of your pocket to maintain a piece of property (hence, "negative" cashflow; positive cashflow is when money goes into your pocket). However, at year end when tax considerations were taken, the tax savings more than made up for the negative cashflow (hopefully), so you ultimately made a profit.

In the past, profits were possible with negative cashflow properties. Because of the changes in the tax laws, however, this is no longer the case. Today, the wise strategy is only to buy properties that do not have negative cashflow. Today, just as when buying stocks, commodities, or anything else, the property must be able to stand on its own. It must be able to make a real profit before taxes.

If we were to pin down the big changes in the tax law to their most direct effect on real estate, I think we would have to examine the term "no negative." It holds the key to making profits in the future.

No Negative

No negative, as we've seen, simply means that a property will, at the least, be able to maintain itself. Let's take a few examples to be sure this is clear.

Negative Cashflow Property

Annual rental income		$10,000
Annual expenses		
Mortgage	$9,000	
Taxes	1,300	

Negative Cashflow Property (*Continued*)

Insurance	300	
Management	600	
Repairs	+1,400	
Total	$12,600	−12,600
Cash loss		$ (2,600)

In this example, the expenses (from whatever source) exceed the income from the property. This calculation is done *before taxes*.

The property shows a $2600 cash loss. In the old days, we could then add depreciation (perhaps $3000 a year) and write off that total $5600 loss ($2600 cash loss plus $3000 depreciation) against our regular income. Assuming a 50 percent tax bracket, that meant a tax savings of $2800. We would lose $2600 on the property, but save $2800 on taxes, for a net gain over the year of $200, as follows:

Cash loss	$2600
Depreciation	+3000
Total write-off	$5600
Tax bracket	×50%
Tax savings	2800
Cash loss	−2600
After-tax cash	$ 200

Today, however, the tax benefits have largely been eliminated, and many of us don't get the second part of that calculation—where the loss on the property is written off against our regular income. This results in the following:

Cash loss	$2600

Today, the calculation is much simpler (assuming we can't get any write-off): The loss is simply a loss. There are no mitigating tax considerations. Assuming we can't write off anything from real estate, it becomes a final out-of-pocket loss. Each year we own this property we lose $2600, or a little better than $200 a month on it. It's as if we bought stocks and, instead of receiving a dividend, we had to pay an extra $200+ a month for the privilege of keeping them.

That's for a negative cashflow property. Now consider a no-negative property.

No-Negative Property

Annual rental income		$10,000
Annual expenses		
Mortgage	$7000	
Taxes	1100	
Insurance	300	
Management	0	
Repairs	+600	
Total	$9000	−9,000
Profit		$1,000

For this property, the expenses (for whatever reason) are significantly less than the rental income. Thus, at the end of the year the property shows an actual profit of $1000. This is cash-in-the-pocket profit. This property not only "maintains" itself (by not requiring us to put in additional cash), but also gives us back a return.

The Difference Between the Two Properties

In the old days, we were concerned about tax shelters. Investors wanted loss from real estate (preferably paper loss, such as came from depreciation) so that they could reduce their taxes on ordinary income. Properties that regularly lost money were considered beneficial, not detrimental.

Today, however, the situation is reversed. With the tax benefits eliminated, or at least significantly reduced, investors can no longer look for tax shelters. Rather, the property today must stand on its own. It must not show a cash loss. It must not require additional out-of-pocket support (negative cashflow) from the investor. To my way of thinking, if, in today's world, you're taking money out of your pocket each month to support a property and you've got no tax advantages to offset it, you've got a loser!

Of course, the argument could be raised that there are many people who still qualify for the $25,000 tax shelter. Can't they afford a bit of negative cashflow since they can still write it off their taxes?

My answer here is twofold. First, remember that the portion of the write-off that we take (if we qualify) is actually a deferral. That deferred income will eventually come back as ordinary income. Thus, the apparent advantage of the $25,000 allowance may be largely illusory.

Second, if you buy a property counting on writing off that negative cashflow, what happens if either (1) Congress eliminates it next year or (2) your own income rises and you lose the allowance?

Today, the prudent investor will forget about the tax shelter aspects of real estate. Even if you are entitled to them *now*, you may just be digging a hole into which to fall if the laws are tightened further in the future.

New Game—New Strategies

It can't be said enough: Whether you're a big or a small investor, to make money in real estate today, you have to buy properties that make money (or at least don't lose money). Financial advisors have long told investors to buy only real estate that makes good economic sense. The difference is that today these advisors really mean it! The days of the gimmicks are gone.

Three Game Plans That Allow You to Win in Today's Market

It is possible, I believe, to do very well in real estate today. However, to succeed you need to have modern strategies. I liken it to the game of football.

No football coach worth his salt puts a team out on the field without a game plan. That doesn't mean that the game plan will always work. The coach may have to improvise halfway through. But going into the game, there is a plan which, if followed and assuming no unforseen difficulties arise, will allow the team to win under existing conditions.

In real estate today you need a game plan that takes into account the tax reform laws. It's no longer enough simply to find a house that looks cheap, buy it, and then play it by ear. Going into the purchase you need a plan of attack, a method which, if followed (assuming no unforseen difficulties arise), will assure you of a big, healthy profit (otherwise, why invest?).

Here are three game plans which I believe will work in the new real estate market. It really doesn't matter whether you are buying a $10 million office complex or a tiny condo; one of these should apply:

Game Plan 1: Aim for Break-Even

This is the most basic game plan: Only buy properties that will, at the least, break even. They may not show a monthly or even an annual profit, but they won't show a loss, either. At the end of the year, economically speaking, they are a wash. You haven't gotten any return on whatever you put down originally, but you also haven't taken any money out of your pocket to feed negative cashflow.

Put most simply, here's what the figures look like for a typical break-even property:

Break-Even Property

Annual rental income		$10,000
Annual expenses		
Mortgages	$7,500	
Taxes	1,500	
Insurance	300	
Management	0	
Repairs	+700	
Total	$10,000	−10,000
Cashflow		$ 0

The property maintains itself without any additional infusion of capital. (Later in the book we'll go into the many ways of judging a property to determine if it will break even. Also, in Appendix A is a fill-in evaluation sheet you can use for properties you are considering.)

What's the advantage of a break-even in real estate? The goal behind this game plan is ultimately to win through appreciation. Over time, the tenants will pay down your mortgage and, if you've purchased correctly, the property's value will go up. Eventually, you'll be able to sell or refinance for a big profit.

Another way to think of this plan is like planting a seed. You put it into the ground and wait. Soon a sprig will come up, then a tree, and finally fruit.

Obviously, what we're talking about is long-term investing. This strategy isn't going to work overnight. How long do you have to wait for the fruit? If you're purchasing a house, you should buy with the idea that you will hold the property for 10 years. At that time, you'll either refinance or sell to get back your original investment plus your profit.

(Many financial advisors suggest only anticipating waiting 5 years. It may very well be the case that you can sell profitably after 5, but if your game play calls for 10, you've given yourself an additional margin in case things don't break right early on.)

This is a long-term plan for getting rich. It is mainly useful for young investors who have the time to wait for that big appreciation to occur. The key to it is finding a property that will sustain itself over the long haul. Not every property has long-term staying power. Most do not.

(They have big expenses in the short run.) What it takes is the ability to find and buy correctly using the resources you have. (There's much more about locating appropriate properties in Chapter 5.)

Game Plan 2: Hold for Rental Income

Rental properties are back and with them a strategy that investors would never have dreamed of just a few years ago. The impetus was all toward tax shelters. Today, however, this option suddenly makes very good sense.

To hold for rental income, you buy a house, condo, or more likely, a small apartment building where the rental income is higher than *all* expenses. This gives you a monthly return on your investment. Here's what a typical Game Plan 2 property might look like:

Positive Cashflow Property

Annual rental income		$25,000
Annual expenses		
Mortgage	$11,000	
Taxes	3,000	
Insurance	600	
Management	2,200	
Repairs	+2,200	
Total	$19,000	−19,000
Positive cashflow		$ 6,000

Here the property does more than break even—it makes money. In this example, the property has a positive cashflow of $500 per month.

Now, you may indeed be able to sell profitably sometime in the future, but that is not your primary goal. Your primary goal is to get income out of the property. In many ways it's like investing money in a certificate of deposit (CD). You invest your money, then receive monthly checks.

Instead of interest, however, you get rental income, with a big difference. With a CD the interest remains constant. With a property, over a period of time you should be able to increase rents, giving you an escalating income. In addition, assuming the property value goes up, you are also getting some capital appreciation. Bought right, this method makes far better sense from a profit perspective than most conservative cash investments.

This method is particularly suited to older investors who have accumulated a substantial amount of capital and want a steady cashflow to live on without eroding that capital.

The key, however, is having a large amount of cash. You're simply not going to be able to get a big, positive cashflow with minimum down payments. Given today's market, you'll have to plan to put down *at least* 25 percent to get the desired results. However, with an appropriate down payment, the return (with relative security) on your money can be fabulous. If you have the money to sock away, certainly consider buying a property before automatically sticking it in a CD.

Game Plan 3: Go for the Quick Turnover

Every football game has its razzle-dazzle plays. Going for quick turnovers (buying and then selling almost immediately) in today's market is as razzle-dazzle as you get in real estate. It means throwing caution (and your capital and credit to boot!) to the winds. You're the daring player who bets it all on one quick touchdown play. You're going to buy a house and resell it, often before escrow closes (i.e., before you take title or possession)!

This plan, is for seasoned investors, or at least those who are quite familiar with the real estate market in which they are dealing.

You can win very big and very fast here. But, you can also lose just as quickly—and the stakes can be high. While the first two game plans are conservative and usually involve investing capital over a long period of time, here your capital (hopefully) is tied up only a short time.

The idea is to find a property so low priced that you can buy it and then resell it (often right out of escrow!) for a whopping big profit. You become a speculator in property just the way others speculate in stocks or commodities.

You don't think properties exist that can be turned over quickly for profit? Think again. Every area of the country has some of these being sold every day. The only trick is knowing where and by whom. Often, very little to no capital is needed! We'll have more to say on this later in the book.

The Importance of No Negative Cashflow

These, then, are the three game plans that you can employ to make money in real estate in today's market. Notice that in each of the game plans there is one common thread: no negative cashflow. To state it plainly and simply, if you're taking money out of your pocket each month to support a property, in today's world you've got a loser! That's why these three game plans work.

To my way of thinking, "no negative" is the real estate buzz word for the remainder of this decade. Investors who buy property with no negative cashflow will prosper. Those who buy with negative cashflow will lose. To a very large extent, in fact, the entire purpose of this book is to show you how to buy properties that have no negative. (The clock has turned back!)

Why Even a Little Negative Cashflow Hurts

Having gone to some length to emphasize that negative cashflow hurts, I'm going to take it a wee bit further. My reasoning here is simple—when you go out to look at property, you are going to be bombarded by brokers and sellers who tell you something like this: "This is a great property. So what if it has only a little negative cashflow? That'll probably correct itself in a few years. Don't worry about the negative—it's small potatoes." When this happens, I want you to know without any doubt why even a small amount of negative cashflow is bad.

We'll assume that you are considering buying a property that you will hold long-term for appreciation (Game Plan 1) purposes. (For Game Plan 2, only positive cashflow properties would be considered, and for Game Plan 3, the cashflow is considered only in terms of risk, since you hope to resell very quickly. Hence, here we're talking only about property held long-term—Game Plan 1.) In order to purchase the property, you will have to put up $5000 in cash of your own money for the down payment and the closing costs. Here's the way the property cashflow will then look:

Property Being Considered

Annual rental income		$7500
Annual expenses		
Mortgage	$6000	
Taxes	1000	
Insurance	300	
Management	400	
Repairs	+1000	
Total	$8700	−8700
Cashflow		$(1200)

This property has a relatively low capital investment. Perhaps it's in a good area with a good tenant base. There's just one catch, however. You'll be required to come up with $100 negative cashflow a month.

"It's only a hundred bucks," the agent says with a look that expresses "How petty can you be?" You say to yourself, "That isn't much. I'll take it."

Stop! Consider. Let's take a closer look. If you have to pay just $100 per month out of pocket to maintain a property for 10 years (remember, Game Plan 1 calls for long-term thinking—we're not talking about quick turnaround property here) you've invested an additional $12,000 cash in the property *plus* compounded interest you might otherwise have received on that money. In reality, $100 a month invested in a savings account at 7 percent compounded over 10 years is $17,740.31. Suddenly your capital investment may be much higher than you might have thought. Instead of an investment of just $5000, you've got an investment of closer to $23,000.

It gets worse. You get nothing back on either your initial investment or any negative cashflow *until* you refinance or sell 5 to 10 years down the road.

Remember, your goal was to plant a seed and let it grow, to come back years later and reap what was sowed. Your goal was not to keep sowing in the same field. If all you've invested is the initial $5000, that's not so terrible. You plant $5000 and come back 5 to 10 years later and have $20,000 or more. Who's complaining?

However, if you have to add money each month, things don't work out quite so well. By having to add money each month, you could end up putting in more than $20,000 only to get $20,000 out. That hardly makes much sense.

Additionally, there's the psychological drain. For most investors, having a negative cashflow property, even one with just $100 a month negative, is more than their psyches can bear. There's something that tears at the spirit when we have to dig into our pockets *every month* for years without ever seeing the return. Quite frequently, investors who have negative cashflow simply sell at a loss within 2 to 3 years. They just want out from under the negative—at any price. (And remember, that loss may not be deductible.)

If you want to know the meaning of the word *alligator* in real estate, just get a property that constantly runs a negative cashflow. (An alligator just keeps on eating away at you.)

Finally there is the risk. Our goal is eventually to refinance or sell at a profit. But there's no guarantee that even with the best of planning we'll be able to do that.

Real Estate Does Not Always Go Up in Value

If you think that property has to go up in value over 10 years, just ask the farmers in the Midwest about their homes and land. Roughly half the country is still agricultural. And between 1982 and 1986 it lost better than 40 percent of its value.

Or ask the people who abandoned their homes in Houston. Whole tracts, often only 2 or 3 years old, became worthless. The drop in oil prices during 1985 and 1986 caused mass unemployment and drove people out. Investors as well as homeowners simply abandoned their property. Often within weeks, vandalism turned houses into worthless hulks. Property values dropped by more than 60 percent in some areas of Texas, Oklahoma, and other oil patch states. (And back in 1980, Houston was touted as the *best* real estate opportunity area in the country by many "experts"!)

This is not to say that all real estate investing is bad. During the same period, prices appreciated dramatically on both coasts. It's just to say that there is risk.

What we are risking (besides our credit rating) is our capital. In the previous example, if our only investment is the $5000 down payment, that's our total risk. If things don't work out, then that's all we've lost.

But just a small negative cashflow like $100 a month substantially increases our risk. Suddenly, over a period of years we can stand to lose as much as $20,000 or more.

Negative cashflow enormously increases what we have at risk. It challenges the very soundness of our investment.

In our post–Tax Reform Act era, negative cashflow should be the most feared aspect of real estate. I can't emphasize this enough. If there's only one criterion by which you judge the purchase of a piece of property, let it be the cashflow. Avoid like the plague properties with negative cashflow.

Problems with Nothing-Down Properties

Some readers may notice that one recently popular strategy is notably missing from our game plans—buying with "no down payment."

No-down buying of real estate, contrary to what some outside the field have suggested, definitely is possible. I have done it as have thousands of others. However, to hark back to Ecclesiastes, "To every thing there is a season, and a time to every purpose under the heaven." (3:1). Generally speaking, now is not the time and most areas of the country are not the places for no-down-payment purchases.

No-down buying was popularized in both books and seminars at a time, several years ago, when the real estate market was exceedingly hot. Properties were turning over quickly in virtually all parts of the country. Prices were soaring.

In a hot market, be it real estate or anything else, the fastest way to make money is to get control of as much of the market as possible with as little of your own money as possible. Tie up properties, any properties, and then just wait. Soon the price goes up and you resell. If you don't use any money of your own and you resell for a profit of $5000, the return is incredible!

But, it only works when prices go up quickly and you don't hold onto the property for long. When prices go up slowly or stay constant or (worst-case scenario) decline, buying property for no down payment is another matter. The reason, once again, is negative cashflow. As we'll see in a few paragraphs, buying with no down payment almost invariably results in a large negative cashflow.

If you have to hold onto that property for years waiting for prices to go up, you could end up investing far more through negative cashflow than you would ever have had to invest by just paying a normal down payment.

Nothing down only makes sense if you can find sellers willing to sell cheaply in a quick and hot market. As of this writing, however, the market is not that way. Buying with no down payment and then holding the property for a long time can be nothing short of a disaster.

The Law of Negative Cashflow in No-Down Properties

I would be all for buying properties for long-term investment with no cash down *if* the purchase could be arranged so that there was no negative cashflow. Unfortunately, unless the seller is a fool and gives the property away for far less than it's worth (something that rarely happens these days), negative cashflow almost always occurs.

Here's the reason: Investment properties, in reality, are often priced not on the basis of what a buyer will pay, but on the basis of what a lender will loan. And lenders, being relatively shrewd in the short term, will usually lend no more than can be paid back from the cashflow of the property.

This is obvious with large properties, such as apartment or office buildings, for which the sales price is directly related to the rental income. It's not at all obvious with regard to single-family houses or condos, but, surprisingly, it still applies.

Thus, if a house has a loan on it for $80,000, chances are that, in an average deal, any cashflow from rents will be just enough to pay back that $80,000. In a well-structured deal, the cashflow will pay back the loan amount plus taxes, insurance, and some maintenance. In a superior deal, the cashflow will cover all expenses plus provide a small, positive cashflow. Thus, the mortgage (along with other costs) tends to eat up all or most of the cashflow in nearly all normal deals.

Now consider a nothing-down deal. Here, in addition to the normal mortgage amount, the buyer is also financing the down payment. That means that, in addition to all the other carrying costs, the buyer also has to pay the cost of that 10 to 20 percent he or she would normally have put down. On a house with an $80,000 mortgage, a sales price would usually be around $100,000 (mortgages are typically 80 percent of sales price), with the buyer putting down $20,000. If the buyer doesn't put down that $20,000 (and the seller doesn't give away the house for free), then the down has to be financed.

(Don't be deluded into thinking that the down payment does not have to be financed. The down must come from somewhere. Either it's a mortgage paid each month, or it's a note deferred to sometime in the future, or its some other device. But the piper must be paid. The down must exist someplace.)

When a down is financed, money has to be obtained (often on a monthly basis) to pay it. Almost always that money comes out of the buyer's pocket. It's called negative cashflow.

A no-down-payment deal that goes long-term usually ends up with massive negative cashflow coming from carrying charges on financing the down. Either the buyer must now "walk" and leave the deal behind (these days, credit agencies are getting quite sophisticated in tracking such buyers) or must put in increasing amounts of capital, often exceeding what would have been the normal down payment.

If we were to plot the cashflow on a property in terms of financing, it would generally look like that in Figure 3.1. Note that in the range of about 80 percent of value, most properties turn from positive cashflow to negative. At 100 percent financing, almost all properties perform negatively.

In the past, if you bought with no down payment and got caught having to hold the property for a long time, at least you could write off the negative cashflow, making up for most if not all of the loss through tax savings. With the tax reform, however, that's no longer an option. Today, loss is really loss.

To my way of thinking, trying to buy with no down in today's new post–tax shelter market is a prescription for disaster. The person today who buys with no down payment, one way or another, usually ends up with an alligator.

Beware of Nothing-Downers

Don't be swayed by supposed gurus who tell you that you can have your cake and eat it, too; that you can buy property for *both* no negative *and* no down payment. Theoretically, it is true that you can do it, but your chances of finding that kind of deal are about as good as growing orchids in Anchorage.

I personally have met too many people suffering the burdens of trying to dispose of alligator properties they bought for no down payment to have any sympathy for those who advocate it. Nothing down has become an anachronism—a gimmick for which the time is long past.

The Bottom Line

The new tax laws have changed the face of real estate in the United States, perhaps forever. The old days of throwing money at property and knowing that even if you got a bad deal, it would be a good deal because of the tax treatment, are long gone.

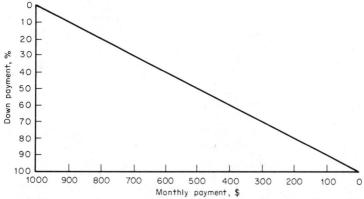

Figure 3.1 Increasing the down payment will significantly reduce the monthly mortgage payment.

Today, prices are indeed appreciating in many areas of the country and rental rates are going up, all of which means that it is still possible to make good money investing. But, as we've seen, you've got to do it right. You have to have a game plan that involves no negative cashflow.

In the next chapter, we'll see how a deal can be structured to avoid negative cashflow and, after that, how to find properties that fit.

4

How to Select Property That Will Make Money

As we've seen, what counts today is the real return on a piece of real estate. In this chapter, we are going to see how to structure a deal so that we can buy a property with no negative cashflow—one that will provide a real return. (If you have any doubts as to why we want to buy without negative cashflow, reread the last two chapters!)

How to Evaluate Property That Will Give Positive Return

In one respect, we are putting the cart before the horse. Normally we have a property in mind before we start worrying about how to structure the deal to purchase it.

Here, however, we are concerned with proper structuring first. The reason for this turnabout is simple. The new tax laws mean that we have to evaluate properties differently than in the past. Today, we have to look at the economics of a property, any property, as the first part of our decision to buy. (We no longer can go for just a good location.) Therefore, before considering specific properties, let's begin by seeing what would make *any* property a good deal.

The Four Ratios That Show You've Got a Good Deal

It is possible to hire an analyst to spend several weeks evaluating the economics of a property. However, if we're buying a single house or condo, that's hardly practical. Therefore, I've reduced the basic evaluation process down to four simple ratios that anyone can remember and keep in the back of his or her mind. If you remember these four ratios and apply them the next time you look at a property, you'll find that you won't go far wrong. The ratios are:

Income/Expense

Price/Rent

Cashflow/Total Income

Cashflow/Investment Capital

Don't be intimidated if you don't understand any of these ratios. They are all really quite simple and easy to apply. We'll consider each of them separately.

Income/Expense Ratio

This is just an easy way of reminding us to be sure that the property is at least break-even. It compares the income from rents on a property to the total of expenses. The ratio is found by dividing the income by the expenses.

$$\text{Ratio} = \frac{\text{income}}{\text{expenses}}$$

Thus, if the income is $1000 and the expenses are $950, the ratio is 1.053 ($1000 divided by $950 = 1.053). Anything better than 1 is break-even and means that the property is at least potentially viable. To get no negative cashflow, the ratio should be 1 or higher.

The real trick, of course, is knowing what the true income and the true expenses are. Anyone who has invested in real estate over a period of time will quickly tell you that finding true income can be exceedingly deceptive.

True expenses can be equally baffling, particularly allowances for maintenance and repairs. Later, we'll examine in detail how to find both. For now, however, just keep in mind that the ratio of expenses to income must be 1 or greater for the property to make economic sense in today's market (the higher the number the better).

Price/Rent Ratio

This is an old rule of thumb that's been used for years to help determine whether or not the purchase price is appropriate. Basically, it says that the monthly income from rents should be not less than 1 percent of the total purchase price. (The ratio just correlates the monthly rent with the price of the property.) If the monthly rent is less than 1 percent, the property is too expensive (from an economic no-negative perspective).

$$\text{Ratio} = \frac{\text{purchase price}}{\text{monthly rent}}$$

The ratio resulting from this division should be 100 or less. If it is, chances are that the property will have at least a break-even on cashflow. If the number is higher than 100, the chances are that there will be a negative cashflow.

It's important to remember that this is a rule of thumb. A lot depends on how the financing is structured as well as on other aspects of the deal. But, in general, the ratio works surprisingly well. Let's take an example. We find a condo that is selling for $100,000. We determine the true monthly rent (using a method from the next chapter) to be $950. Is the purchase price too high or is it okay?

$$\frac{100,000}{950} = 105$$

The ratio is over 100, so it is too high. Chances are we'll have negative cashflow. What's the more correct price? Multiply the monthly rent ($950) by 100. The more correct price would be $95,000.

If you've never used this ratio, it's sure to be a revelation to you. And old-timers will assure you that the best part about it is that it usually does work. It's a great way to determine if you'd be paying too much (economically speaking) for a property.

Cashflow/Total Income Ratio

This is another easy-to-understand, easy-to-use ratio. It compares the total amount of positive cashflow (if any) to the total income from the property. It looks like this:

$$\text{Ratio} = \frac{\text{cashflow}}{\text{total income}}$$

The purpose here is to determine just how fragile or secure is your cashflow on the property. If you're going to be using the cashflow as income on which to live or even if you're just treating it as profit, it's important that you know at the onset how likely you are to collect it each month.

The best way to see how this ratio works is to take an exaggerated example. Let's say we are considering buying a house on which the monthly positive cashflow will be $100. We also have a large apartment building to consider on which the positive cashflow is exactly the same, $100. Which is the more secure cashflow? This formula tells you.

House	Apartment complex
$\dfrac{\$100 \text{ cashflow}}{\$500 \text{ income}} = 0.20 \ (20\%)$	$\dfrac{\$100 \text{ cash flow}}{\$5000 \text{ income}} = 0.02 \ (2\%)$

The higher the ratio, the more secure the cashflow. In both cases, the positive cashflow is $100. But, in the case of the house, the positive cash-flow is a full 20 percent of the total rental income. In the case of the apartment complex it is only 2 percent. An unexpected expense high enough to wipe out the cashflow is far more likely to occur in a property for which the cashflow is only 2 percent of the total rental income than on a property for which it is 20 percent. Another way of saying this is: In the apartment building we may have 10 units, each paying $500. The chances that there will be a $100-a-month additional expense there is far greater than if we have only one unit (the house) paying $500. (To be comparably safe, the apartment building should have a $1000 positive cashflow, or 20 percent.)

Of course, in real life it's rare that we would compare apartment buildings with houses. That's sort of like comparing apples and oranges. But we might compare two houses, each with different cashflows and incomes. This formula gives us a way to see just how secure the cashflow is in each case.

Cashflow/Investment Capital Ratio

In the past, the return on capital on real estate was difficult to calculate because of the tax shelters available. If we forget about the tax shelter however (assuming it's a bonus, if we get it), the return is much easier to figure.

This ratio isn't concerned with the return *of* our capital or with any profit we might make when we sell or refinance sometime in the future. It is only concerned about the return *on* our capital. It expresses the same sort of figure we would get if we had invested our money in a CD in a bank.

$$\text{Return on investment} = \frac{\text{cashflow} \times 12}{\text{total capital investment}}$$

Let's say our positive cashflow is $100 a month. We multiply this by 12 to get $1200 annually, and divide by our total investment, which we'll say is $10,000. What is the monthly cash return on our investment?

$$\$100 \times 12 = \frac{\$1,200}{\$10,000} = 0.12 \ (12\%)$$

As can be seen, $100 a month positive cashflow on a $10,000 investment isn't bad. It gives us 12 percent on our money. Even $100 per month positive cashflow on a $20,000 investment (6 percent) would equal some savings account interest rates as of this writing, illustrating that even a modest positive cashflow will give us a strong return on our investment. This ratio allows us to see exactly what it is. (Of course, the true return will ultimately be realized when we sell the property and reap our full profit. This is just the ongoing return.)

When to Use the Ratios

Use these ratios whenever you are considering the purchase of any real estate. They will tell you whether you will have a positive cashflow, how secure it will be, and what kind of a return it will give you on your investment.

Of course, there are many other formulas that sophisticated real estate analysts use (such as the internal rate of return, the discounted value of the investment, and others), but these are complex formulas and often the results are difficult for the small investor to apply. If you're looking for simplicity, stick with these four. You won't go far wrong with them.

Buying Right

The above four formulas will help you determine if you've got a good deal. But they won't tell you how to get a good deal. We'll go into that now.

A good deal in real estate today depends on how it is structured. Move a few elements around, change a figure here or there, and a moribund project comes to life—or a viable project sinks below the sunset. Here we're going to examine the factors that comprise a deal and how they can be manipulated to (hopefully) improve it.

How to Figure Out the Expenses

There are just so many factors that make up any real estate deal, and they go on two different sides of the page. On one side are factors that influence income; on the other side are factors that influence expenses.

Income in real estate is usually from only one source: rent. We've already touched upon income and stated that we'll deal with it at length in the next chapter. Here, therefore, we'll concentrate on expenses. These are the typical factors that influence the monthly/annual expenses on any piece of real estate:

1. Price

2. Down payment

3. Mortgage

4. Insurance

5. Taxes

6. Repairs required on building

7. Maintainability of property

8. Ease of renting

Each is a factor that should be addressed *at the time of purchase*, because it will directly affect expenses later on. (Don't make the mistake of thinking you won't have to worry about one or more of these, such as repairs or management. Even if you do repair work yourself, there are still expenses: the cost of replacement parts, of advertising, of renting repair equipment, and so on, not to mention the value of your own time.)

The goal, of course, is to get expenses as low as possible. The lower the expenses, the more likely they are to be less than income and, therefore, to produce a positive cashflow. How do we do it? How do we manipulate these factors at the time we purchase the property in order to be sure that our expenses will be sufficiently low to get no negative cashflow later on?

Variable Versus Fixed Expenses

At the onset, it's important to understand that there are some factors about which we can do nothing at the time of purchase (except recognize them for what they are). Here are the factors about which we generally can do nothing. They should be considered "fixed."

1. Insurance
2. Taxes
3. Repairs required on building
4. Maintainability of property
5. Ease of renting

Insurance is insurance. The lender will require it even if for some foolish reason we decided to waive it. We may have some flexibility in choosing a less expensive liability policy, but not much. Taxes, similarly, are something over which we normally have no control.

Repairs to put the property into shape will determine how much additional cash we need to come up with (if any) before we can get tenants. Unless we have a "fixer-upper" in bad shape, this is usually a relatively small amount. But, if the property needs repairs, they will have to be done at whatever the cost. We may save a bit of money by shopping around or by doing it ourselves. Either way, however, it will cost something—a fixed amount that, with experience, we should be able to estimate fairly accurately before we buy.

Maintainability has to do with the age of the property and the kind of neighborhood it's in. Older properties cost more to maintain. Any property more than 10 years old will have constant problems, from broken water heaters to collapsed garage door hinges, from leaking faucets to shorted-out light fixtures. The older the building, the greater the costs of maintaining it. The neighborhood will determine if we have vandalism and are constantly repairing broken windows or washing away graffiti.

There's nothing we can do about this maintainability, except buy a newer property. If we have an older property, we'll just have to count on a higher maintenance expense.

Ease of renting has to do with the location. Some properties have a large supply of potential tenants nearby; others do not. I once bought a property where the only possible tenants came from a nearby nuclear power plant. It was a good supply, but limited. They could only afford a particular price range and they tended to be transferred regularly, meaning there was a high turnover.

There was nothing I could do about this. The costs of rerenting (cleaning up, advertising, showing, changing locks, and so forth) were going to be high on the property no matter what.

Taxes, insurance, initial repairs, maintainability, and ease of renting are all relatively fixed factors over which we have little control (except to go elsewhere). The best we can do is make our best guess about what they will realistically be and go from there.

There are, however, three variable factors which can dramatically influence the expenses on the property: the price, the down payment, and the financing.

Price

A lower price automatically means reduced expenses: a lower mortgage, lower taxes, and lower insurance. Those all translate into lower monthly payments. Lowering the price is the single biggest factor in cutting costs.

How do we get a lower price? Usually it comes from spending some time searching around *and* by being flexible in what we're willing to accept. It often means buying a property in a less expensive area than where we live. In the next chapter, we'll go into a variety of methods for locating profitable properties in your area.

Down Payment

Increasing the down payment will automatically reduce our expenses. The reason is simple: more down means a lower mortgage. A lower mortgage means less interest to pay and lower monthly payments.

Coming up with more cash for the down payment, however, is usually the most difficult part of buying. Therefore, even though we might feel justified in adding more cash down to reduce our expenses (and ultimately to increase our cashflow), most of us simply are not able to do this.

Realistically speaking, to get any kind of break-even or positive cashflow (to avoid negative cashflow) in almost any deal, we need to put down a minimum of 10 percent and probably closer to 20 percent. This is a rule of thumb, of course, but it's one that's not often far off.

The exception is for those who are looking toward receiving steadily increasing rental income over the years, as in Game Plan 2, described in the last chapter. If you recall, this was suggested as a reasonable operating basis for younger investors with time to wait. Older investors, however, may want to consider buying real estate with much greater down payments: 30 to 50 percent or more.

Increasing the down payment, particularly when interest rates on mortgages are high, will significantly reduce monthly expenses by lowering the monthly payment. Figure 4.1 provides a graphic presentation of how it works.

Financing

Finally, there's financing. This is often the area in which we have the greatest opportunity for manipulation.

We can reduce our mortgage payment (thereby cutting expenses) in a variety of ways, which include finding a lower interest rate, lengthening the term of the mortgage, opting for a balloon payment, or using some other financing strategy.

How to accomplish these techniques is a subject unto itself and will be discussed in Chapter 6.

The Structuring Formula

Getting the good deal, the one without negative cashflow, means structuring the variables correctly. We have just looked at the basics; now let's put them all together.

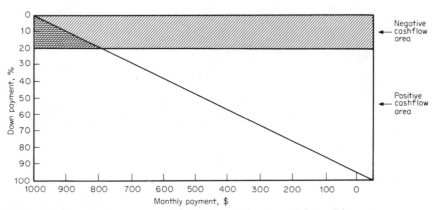

Figure 4.1 How the down payment determines whether the cashflow will be positive or negative.

The following illustrates the *formula for structuring the variables:*

Lower price + higher down payment + high rental income
+ better financing = no negative cashflow

Of course, we are assuming that the fixed expenses noted earlier (taxes, insurance, maintainability, etc.) are reasonable. However, if you keep in mind this simple formula, you'll find that you are soon looking only at economically profitable deals. Other so-called opportunities which seem good on the surface, will quickly fade away.

Having thus obtained the formula for success, how do we start? Where do we find good properties that have lower prices, don't require a lot of repairs, and are easily maintained and easily rented? That's the subject of the next chapter.

5
How to Find Profitable Properties

What is a profitable property? As we've seen, it's one that we can buy and which will have *no negative cashflow*. It's a property that will allow us to use one of the three game plans outlined in the second chapter. It's one that will make us money—big money.

Profitable properties aren't going to be jumping up out at us from behind every bush, asking to be purchased. Rather, we have to do some hunting to find them. In this chapter, we'll examine just where to look and what to look for.

Locating the Contenders

At the onset, it's important to understand that if we go looking for one and only one perfect property, we are going to be disappointed. What we need to do is to develop a list of contenders, half a dozen or more properties that come close to filling our needs. Then we can eliminate the lesser ones and select the best. So the first problem becomes how to find a list of contenders.

Look Close to Home

Painful experience has taught that if you are a small investor in real estate, you *must* look only for properties close to home. Experienced investors will surely nod in agreement, but if you're new to the field, you may be wondering why it's important to buy only close to home. After all, the prices and the financing may be better at some distant location. Even the rental market may be better. And there could be an excellent property management firm willing to find you a property and then handle all management for a nominal fee. Why not opt for properties away from home?

The answer, in a word, is maintenance.

Let's say you are buying a rental property you hope to hang onto for a while and eventually sell for a profit. It's located about a mile from your home.

One evening the tenant calls and says that the light in the kitchen ceiling won't work. She's put in a new bulb, but it still won't go on.

So, you get in your car and you trundle over to the house. After fiddling for a few minutes, you realize that the kitchen light fixture is just an old piece of junk.

You drive over to the local hardware store, buy a new fixture for $15 and return. It takes you perhaps half an hour to install it. The tenant thanks you and you're done with the maintenance. Total cost: $15 and your time.

Now, on the other hand, you've bought another house in another state a thousand miles away. Similarly, the tenant there is having trouble with his kitchen light. But instead of calling you, he calls the property management firm you've hired.

Since it's the evening, no one's there, so he leaves a message on the answering machine and has no light in his kitchen that night.

The next day, the property management firm returns his call, determines the trouble, and says they'll take care of it. An electrician goes out, sees the fixture is too old, and replaces it with a new one. Cost to you: $35 for the fixture, $105 for the electrician, and $10 for the property management firm—for a total of $145.

Of course, you didn't have to do any of the work yourself, which was nice. On the other hand, the tenant is pretty angry because he had no light in the kitchen for two days and he's thinking that the next chance he gets, he might just move.

The Personal Touch

I hope the issues are clear. Renting real estate is very much like tinkering with an old car. There's always something that needs to be fixed. If you hire everything out, it will cost you a fortune and, quite frankly, you may not get the loving service you need. If you do it yourself, on the other hand, it can be fun and inexpensive, particularly if you are the least bit handy.

I personally think this is the least understood aspect of owning just a few rental units by those new to the field. As a landlord, all those little problems with any house become your personal problems. It goes with the territory. While you're watching your house appreciate and those equity dollars increase, you're providing care and maintenance for the property.

The Problem with Being an Absentee Landlord

If you're close by, it's easy. But, personal care is impossible for property that's far away. If you own a house in another state, even if you have the best management company in the world, it's going to cost you money and your tenants are never going to be completely satisfied.

Don't make the mistake of thinking it will be different for you. I know people from California who have bought properties in Arizona and Utah, and even Oklahoma. I know people in New York who have purchased properties in Georgia and in Maine. In *every* case with which I am familiar, the absentee owner complains about the property and is trying, in some cases with difficulty, to get out.

Causing Negative Cashflow

The ultimate result of owning distant property is negative cashflow. Think of it this way: How would it feel if at the end of the month, when you get ready to make your mortgage payment of $622, you open the letter from your property management company and find it contains a check for rental income for $200 and the following note:

> Sorry, but we had to spend $500 this month on new handles for the kitchen stove, fixing the washers in the sink and tub, tacking down the carpet, and scraping some peeling paint off the curb in front.
> I hope we've finally turned the corner on expenses.

That's not an exaggerated note. It was actually sent to an absentee owner. And what could she do, 600 miles away? She could make up the difference out of her pocket, in this case $422 in negative cashflow for that month, and pay the mortgage. (And this on a property that should have been at least break-even!)

The rule is simple: Never, never, never buy property that's far away from home.

How Far Is Too Far?

In my book, *How To Find Hidden Real Estate Bargains* (McGraw-Hill, 1986) I suggest going no further than a 50-mile radius from your home. Since I wrote that, however, I've become a bit more conservative and would suggest a 30-mile radius. If it's more than an hour's drive there and back from your home, it's probably too far to be efficiently rented by you (particularly if you're going to have to show it to prospective tenants).

Locating good properties should be something that you do in your own neighborhood. The minute you wander too far afield, you're asking for trouble.

Look for a Strong Tenant Market

If you're going to be in the real estate rental business, you need tenants. However, unlike some other things, tenants are not always plentiful. Some areas, even those with numerous houses, have relatively few renters. You want an area that is chock full of potential tenants.

For rental houses or condos, generally speaking, a blue-collar area is best. There are two reasons: (1) The tenants tend to be highly employable and, therefore, can pay the rent, and (2) the houses tend to be less expensive than in white-collar areas, hence, you have a better chance of getting the right rental-to-price ratio.

How do you find out if the area you are considering is a good tenant market? There are several ways.

Assuming that you are involved in residential property, first drive around the neighborhoods. If you were going to buy for yourself, you might be looking for such things as beautiful homes and finely manicured yards. You might check shopping and schools. All of these are important, of course, but even more important to you are things that you might not ordinarily want in a neighborhood in which you live. For example, factories, office buildings, commercial buildings, and industrial parks are *good* to have in your area. No, they may not enhance its beauty, but they are sure to provide a steady supply of tenants.

Find out if there's a big employer in the area. Often, whole suburbs will be laid out around a single large company. If that's the case, go to the company's personnel office. Tell them you're going to be offering a rental house and see if they have any lists of house hunters. You may find that they can provide you with a hundred names. Or they may say that they've been laying off lately and may be closing and most of their people are moving out of the area. A quick check could mean the difference between buying and not buying in a particular location.

A Case History

Not long ago I bought a rental home that seemed to be filled with potential. In fact, the potential was so strong that it blinded me to my own advice.

The house was located in the direction of growth of the city. However, it was beyond the city by about 5 miles. A new freeway was being constructed to link the area the house was in to the city proper, but it would be several years before it was done. Until the freeway was built, it was an arduous task getting out to the house over busy surface streets. For this reason, the house was priced 30 percent lower than a comparable home just 5 miles away.

I bought. I assumed that someone would be willing to make the journey as a tenant. All I had to do was keep the property rented and, in a year or two when the freeway opened up the corridor, my property should jump 30 percent or more in value.

The trouble was keeping it rented. Although I had structured the deal so that the property should have no negative, the problem was getting tenants. I couldn't get a steady tenant until I lowered the rent to below the break-even. And there was the increased problem of cleaning up after each tenant.

As of this writing, I still have the property and I keep watching the slow work on that freeway. One day soon, it will open up and, when it does, I should have the option of charging more rent or selling for a substantial profit. But until it does, I'm stuck paying money out of my pocket to keep that property afloat.

Misjudging the tenant market turned a good deal into a marginal one. The tenant market is an essential part of any deal. Don't underestimate it.

Buy Growth

At any given time, some areas are growing and some are decaying. Occasionally they overlap. An old decaying area will suddenly be rejuvenated and come back to life. A healthy growth area will suddenly wither.

If your goal is to make lots of money, forget the areas that are withering. Go for growth. In the years ahead, your decision will pay you back in multiples of what you invest.

The first and perhaps the ultimate real estate investor in this country was John Jacob Astor. More than a century ago, he bought farmland beyond the areas of growth in Manhattan. He always said his only goal in selecting a location was that it was "further out." When the city caught up to where he was, he made his fortune.

Today, it may not be possible to repeat what he did. But it is possible to apply at least the same general principle to your area. Within a 30-mile radius of your own home, there will surely be areas into which the community is growing and other areas which, though they may look good today, are really stagnating. Interestingly enough, the areas of the future are often the least expensive!

Growth is easy to identify. Look for new buildings. New stores, new offices, new houses—all are signs of growth. In almost all areas of the country they follow a pattern, like a wave sweeping across the landscape. See where the wave is going, get in front of it, and you won't go wrong.

Settle Only for a Low Price

Thus far we have been concerned primarily with the overall area. If you have identified an area, it's time to zero in on specific properties. The first thing most of us try to find is a good price. As previously noted, the best way of being assured of getting no negative cashflow is to pay less for the property.

Here are three things to look for when you are shopping for price in real estate:

1. Distressed sellers
2. Distressed properties
3. Repossessions (foreclosures)

Let's consider these one at a time.

The Distressed Seller

This is an individual who is willing to sell the property for what is apparently lower than the going market price. There are always a number of such sellers around. Typically, they must lower their prices because, at the time, the real estate market, is slow. (In a hot market, properties move so quickly that there is no reason for a seller to lower the price.)

Their reasons for selling vary, but usually include the following:

- Transferred
- Divorced
- Lost job
- Death in family
- Can't manage property (if it's a rental)
- Payments are too high

A distressed seller wants out. And he or she wants out right away. Such a seller will not turn down any reasonable offer (and often will not turn down an unreasonable offer, either).

I have a friend who locates distressed sellers. When he goes to the property, he quickly walks through it (having already determined that it's the right area, good tenant market, etc.) and then *on the spot* makes the seller an offer that is, "As is, with all faults, to close in two weeks, for all cash!"

Of course, he has already arranged a line of credit (see the next chapter) so he can pay all cash. And his offer is so low that he figures he can afford to absorb any possible faults that might exist with the property. What his offer does is root out the really motivated sellers. Those who want to get out right now, take it. He's bought a lot of successful properties in this fashion.

Finding Distressed Sellers

Behind every "For Sale" sign, whether by owner or by broker, is a potential distressed seller. You really don't know until you ask. There are, of course, other sources. Here are some you may want to try out:

"For Rent" Listings in Newspapers.   Every landlord is a potential seller. Make up a little card simply asking if the landlord would consider selling the property and use it to respond to "For Rent" listings. You might find a landlord who wants out in the worst way and wants to sell without going through a broker to avoid the fees.

This is particularly true because the Tax Reform Act has provided a special opportunity for small investors. Some big investors bought houses and condos years ago that have produced nothing but negative cashflow during the course of ownership. Suddenly the rules have changed and they want out badly.

It may be possible to buy such properties from distressed landlords at sufficiently reduced prices so that, after you finance them, you show a break-even or even positive cashflow. (The lower price and the refinancing make it happen.)

I know of one enterprising investor who went to his county's hall of records and obtained the name of every absentee landlord in the area. (He determined they were absentee if their mailing addresses were different from the property addresses.) Then he sent each a form letter offering to take the property off their hands.

He mailed the letters out in batches of 100 and got only two or three responses each time. But each response was a potentially good deal for him.

Property Management Firms. These firms always know of some landlords who are anxious to sell. Of course, they usually require a commission paid by the seller, which will be tacked onto the price of the property. But if it's cheap enough, who cares? This is a good way to get unlisted or just-listed property.

Attorneys, Accountants, and Marriage Counselors. These professionals, in their day-to-day work, are in contact with people who, for various reasons, may be forced or are anxious to sell their property. Without betraying any confidence, these professionals may be able either to recommend their client to you or suggest the name of a client you may want to contact directly. This can be an excellent source for reduced-value properties.

Real Estate Brokers. Though this may be surprising to some, often, many real estate brokers would much rather have an outsider buy from a distressed seller a property at a good price than try to buy it themselves. (They may be faced with ethical and legal problems buying their own listings for marked-down prices.) Get to know a goodly number of brokers. Tell them exactly what you are looking for. If they feel you are serious, when something comes up, they'll call.

Go Door to Door. When all else fails, the direct approach always works. Just pick a neighborhood and "farm" it. This is the same thing that real estate agents do. They go knocking on doors, introducing themselves, stating what they want, and just talking to people. Pick a Saturday afternoon. Make copies of a brochure to hand out. It's a grand way to meet people. Those who aren't interested will quickly let you know. But those who are interested will usually be delighted you stopped by, and you could end up with a good property close to home.

Work Your Neighborhood

Not long ago I wanted to pick up a fixer-upper. As previously mentioned, this is a house that is physically run-down. The idea is that, because it's run-down, you pay less. Then you fix it up and, you hope, sell it for a profit.

My method was simple. I drove up and down streets in my own and nearby neighborhoods. Whenever I spotted a house that looked run-down—weeds in front, dilapidated, apparently abandoned—I stopped and left a short note in the door. My note read:

> I'm looking to buy a home that I can fix up in this area. I can pay cash. I can move quickly. If you want a fast sale, please call.
>
> I gave my phone number.

Over a weekend I managed to hand out about ten cards. The results were interesting. One house about four blocks from where I live suddenly got its yard cleaned up and its front painted. I guess the owner felt that if someone coming by thought it was a fixer-upper, he ought to do something to make it look better! If nothing else, my notes helped improve the neighborhood.

I got two calls. Both of these turned out to be disgruntled owners who were indeed intending to sell. But they had inflated ideas about what their properties were worth (more than if they had been fixed up) and neither was under any pressure to sell soon. However, one had a friend who had a distressed property about 2 miles away and he wanted to sell in the worst way. I had found my property.

The message here is simple: If you want to find a distressed property, you need to work the streets. Don't worry. Put in enough time and the right house will find you.

Finding Repossessions

If you don't think that everyone is looking to buy a repo, try this little trick at the next party you attend. Speaking fairly softly and to no one in particular say, "I know of this repo that the bank is trying to unload, if only they could find someone to buy it."

Almost guaranteed you'll soon have an inquiring crowd of people around you. "Repo?" "Bank?" "Unload?" "Tell me more!"

Everyone wants to buy a repossession. The idea is that if you can get a repossessed property, you are getting a bargain, and everyone wants a bargain.

Unfortunately, the truth is often far different than what is imagined. Repossessions are not always wonderful deals. Frequently, in fact, they are terrible deals. The FHA and VA, for example, sell much of their repossessed property at a sort of auction. But they sell it at or higher than market price! Many commercial auction companies likewise dispose of property for high prices.

To be good, a repo must be cheap—cheaper than the market price by far. (Else, it's no advantage to you if you're looking for no negative by getting the price down.)

Three Sources of Repos

If you really want to find a cheap repo, you need to do one of three things: (1) contact a seller and buy the property before the bank forecloses, (2) bid at the foreclosure auction when the bank takes it back, or (3) buy it from the bank after foreclosure.

The first two are not suggested here. In many states, there are laws with severe penalties that apply to speculators who try to "steal" property for low prices from those who are unfortunate enough to be in foreclosure. Unless you know your way around those laws (or have an advisor who does), beware of buying from a seller once the foreclosure has started.

The next opportunity to buy a repo is at the foreclosure sale. The foreclosure procedure involves selling the house "on the courthouse steps" to the highest bidder. However, a person who bids at such a sale is not protected by the niceties of an escrow or of title insurance. Sometimes it is difficult to know whether you are bidding on a first mortgage or a third or fourth mortgage. You could end up spending a lot of money and getting a property that was still mortgaged for more than it was worth!

All of which is to say that unless you know the ropes, stay away from bidding at foreclosure sales. They are tricky, there's lots of money involved, and for the newcomer, there are lots of pitfalls.

That leaves buying a foreclosure from the bank. This is probably your best bet.

The REO Market

REO stands for "real estate owned." It refers to the property that lenders, such as banks and savings and loans (S & Ls), have acquired through foreclosing on bad mortgages.

It's impossible to say how many properties, mostly single-family houses and condos, are at any one time owned by banks and savings and loans because of foreclosure. In a sluggish economy and given the problems in the oil patch and farm belt, as of this writing it's probably close to the half-million mark.

These are properties that lenders have been forced to take back. I say "forced" because the lenders don't want them. They want performing loans. They want borrowers who make their payments on the first of each month. They don't want houses and condos that simply sit there on the books. The lenders are very anxious to get rid of these real estate–owned, or REO, properties.

However, the banks and the savings and loans are caught in a dilemma. If they go public and advertise for sale all the properties they have, they'll hurt the retail market by diluting it with properties and they'll tarnish their own image by admitting they made a number of bad loans.

Consequently the REO market is hidden. It's hidden from all but those who make it their business to find out about it. That should be you.

Finding REOs

The best way to find out about the REO market is to contact your own bank or savings and loan and simply ask to talk to the REO officer. You'll probably be sent back toward the main office and then, if you're lucky, someone from the REO department will come on the phone.

The REO officer, if he or she doesn't know you, will be suspicious. Yes, they want to dump properties, but they don't want bad publicity. Yes, they want legitimate buyers, but they don't want to sell to someone who will not make the payments and dump the property back on them again.

At this point, truth is your best weapon. Your best chance of finding out about an REO is to tell the officer why you want one (for investment), as specifically as possible the area in which you want it, and the price range in which you are looking.

If you're ever going to get an REO officer to tell you about a property or two, this is your chance. You haven't asked the lender *how many REOs* they have or *where* they are all located (questions that could be embarrassing to the lender). You've only asked if they have any in a specific price range and location. If they have, chances are they'll tell you.

If you're told, then your job is easy. Just go out and look at them. If they don't have any or they won't tell you, just look in a phone book and find another lender to try. (There are lots of lenders with REOs these days.)

Negotiating for an REO

Once you find an REO that you like, buying it is much like buying any other property. You make an offer subject to certain terms. Usually, but not always, the lender is willing to carry back the financing, often at better-than-market terms. If the property needs work, you may be able to specify that the lender pay you a certain amount (possibly thousands of dollars) as you complete the work.

Finally, there's price. The lender, like any seller, wants the best price. However, if you're the only buyer to come by this week and the house or condo has been sitting on the books for a long time, you might get a terrific price.

No long ago I bought an REO from a large savings and loan association. It was a difficult purchase because the house was located in a very desirable area (although it was in terrible shape).

The S & L's appraisers had determined its value at $115,000 "as is." That was roughly $30,000 below market. But it had probably $10,000 worth of repair work that needed doing.

I found out about the property in the morning, saw it at noon, and went in before 3 o'clock to make my offer. I was going to offer $105,000. But when I got there I found I was third in line. There were two offers ahead of mine!

So I offered full price. (Interestingly, the first person also offered full price and the second person offered $2000 *above* what the S & L was asking!) The S & L took the highest offer (not mine). I was disappointed, but forgot the property and continued looking for other REOs.

About two weeks later I got a call from the S & L. The buyer with the offer above asking price hadn't qualified for the loan, so he was out. The other buyer had bought a different property, so she was no longer interested. Did I want it and, if I did, could I be there within half an hour? My answers were "Yes" and "Yes." So I got the REO, fixed it up, rented it out, and as of this writing, it brings in $182 positive cashflow monthly (plus being worth much more than I put into it).

Another Way to Find REOs

If trudging around to various S & Ls doesn't appeal to you, there's the alternative of using an REO service. These are available in most large metropolitan areas, but they are expensive—often over $100 a month. They are just a newsletter that picks up all the foreclosures, which must be published in a legal newspaper. But they give you location and lender. You can check out the properties first. Then, after you find one you like, you can go directly to the lender.

REOs are an excellent way of picking up properties cheaply. But they do require legwork. Here, it's a matter of putting a little sweat in before you get the profit out.

Distressed sellers, distressed properties, and repos—these, then, are the keys to finding properties with low prices.

Get the True Rental Rate

Once you've finally located a property that you think is going to be a terrific no-negative investment for you, there's an important additional step you must take. You must determine the *true* rental rate.

Some readers, I'm sure, are wondering why I'm emphasizing the word *true*. Does that imply that there's a false rental rate?

The answer is yes, it does! The false rental rate is that rate for which you can rent the property as told you by anyone else. In other words, a wise investor is a skeptic. Never, never, never take anyone's word for what the rental rate may be.

Here's an example. Not long ago I purchased a property in an area in which I was unfamiliar with rents. I bought the property from a previous investor who told me that she was sure it could be rented for $900 a month (although it was then currently vacant).

The property was a mess and desperately needed repairs and clean-up; hence, it couldn't be rented quickly and there was no way actually to determine what rent it would bring when fixed up.

The owner had originally bought it as a tax shelter. She wanted out, and I got a good price. My payments ended up being $900 a month, so, according to her estimate of the rental rate, it should be a break-even.

But the most I could rent it for, as is, was $700 a month, or $200 negative. I moved a tenant in at once at that rate with the understanding that the rate was going up to $900 as soon as the place was fixed up. It was understood that the only reason the rent was less was because of the condition. The tenant agreed to do some of the clean-up work required while I came in and did much of the repairs.

It took several months. Eventually the house was in shape and the rent went up to $900. The tenant immediately moved out, complaining the rent was too high.

So, I put the house up for rent at $1000 a month. It rented within 3 days. Currently I have it rented for $1050, for a strong, positive cash-flow.

The moral here is that the true rent is what you can get, not what anyone says you can get.

Finding the True Rental Income

There are several ways of determining the true rental income from a property. The most frequently used, if the property is currently rented, is to take the current rental rate. That is demonstrably the income that the property will produce.

But, is it rented below market, as can sometimes be the case (see the last example)? Has it been rented to a relative of the former owner who is paying an inflated rent, part of which is then refunded under the table so as to inflate the apparent income? (Don't laugh, it happens!) If that's the case, the true rental rate may be much lower. What if the property has never been rented before (or you don't know and can't find out what the previous rental rate was)? What do you do then?

Finding the rental rate now requires some legwork on your part. But, I can assure you from hard-won experience, it's worth the time.

First, check the local papers.

That's where landlords advertise for tenants. If you're renting a house, look for houses for rent in your area that have the same number of bedrooms, bathrooms, and amenities as does yours.

Then, go look at at least three rentals.

This is where the legwork comes in. You're gathering information and you can't get it sitting at home with your feet up reading a book like this. See what the rental market is like, firsthand. See what else is out there. When you do, be sure to ask:

1. How long has this been for rent?
2. Is the landlord paying anything extra (like utilities)?
3. What kind of security deposit and lease are required?
4. And, of course, what is the amount of the rent?

Compare the houses you see with the one you're considering.

(Remember that tenants go for cleanliness. A clean house rents faster, though not necessarily for more.)

This comparison will quickly give you an idea of the rental market, and you should be able to approximate the amount for which you can rent your particular house. But again, this will not give you the *true* rental rate.

Here's the reason: If you have only one house (or condo) to rent, you have a unique situation. It's not as if you're trying to rent one of sixty apartments. Yours is one of a kind.

Depending on the condition, location, availability of tenants, and availability of other properties *at the precise time you are renting* you may get more or less than the so-called market price. You won't know until you try.

The *true rent* for a property, ultimately, is the most you can get for it.

My experience has shown that the best way to approach the problem is to comparison shop, see what the rent on the property was before (if it was rented), and then reduce the figure by 5 percent. If the apparent rent you can get is $1000, feel fairly confident that you can rent the place for $950.

Then, if that rent makes sense in terms of positive cashflow, buy the property and, when it comes time to rent it out, try to get 5 percent more than the market—in this case, $1050.

Try it for a few weeks. If there are no takers, drop your price by 5 percent. If there are still no takers, drop it by another 5 percent. By now, you should be 5 percent below the so-called market rate and able to rent it instantly. And, because this was the rent calculated for purposes of determining cashflow, you should still have at least a break-even. (We'll have more to say about renting in Chapter 8.)

It Takes Work

Locating profitable properties takes work. But that work needn't be discouraging *if* you remember that the properties are indeed out there waiting to be discovered. It's not like you're looking for a needle in a haystack. You're looking for an opportunity in your own or a nearby neighborhood. Opportunities crop up all the time—and they go to the investor who is most vigilant.

6
Tips and Techniques in Financing

Everyone knows what the best financing is; it's the financing that translates into the lowest monthly payment.

The lowest monthly payment gives us the best chance of getting no negative cashflow. The single highest monthly expense item in real estate is the mortgage payment. Reduce that payment and expenses swiftly go down. Reduce it far enough and the income from rents soon will reach break-even or better.

Our goal in this chapter is to explore real estate financing from the perspective of getting the lowest possible monthly payment. Hopefully, you'll come across some techniques here that help you determine the difference between a good deal and no deal.

(In this chapter, it's assumed that the reader has some idea of the basics of real estate finance. If you're new to the field, I suggest reading one of the many good books that explain real estate financing in detail, as does my own, *Making Mortgages Work For You,* McGraw-Hill, 1987).

1. Go for the Longer-Term Mortgage

Today, lenders usually offer two basic terms: 15 and 30 years. To induce borrowers to go for the shorter term, the 15-year mortgages often have an interest rate ½ to 1 percent lower than the 30-year term. Many brokers and financial planners advise going for the shorter term to get the better rate.

My advice is to go for the longer-term, slightly higher-interest-rate mortgage. Here's why:

To begin, we want the lowest possible monthly payment to help achieve no negative cashflow. A 30-year loan at even a 1 percent higher interest rate always has a lower payment than a 15-year loan with a 1 percent lower interest rate. And the difference will be significant: the total monthly payment for the 15-year mortgage will be more than 10 percent higher. To avoid negative cashflow, we want lower monthly payments. Go for the longer term.

I can hear accountants grinding their teeth. Why pay the extra interest? In a 15-year loan, much more of the payment goes to principal. If we keep the property for 10 years, over the course of a 15-year loan, half the mortgage will be paid off. Over a 30-year loan, only about 15 percent will be paid off. Why go for the longer term? It makes no economic sense.

For those who aren't sure of the argument, consider the graph in Figure 6.1. It shows the amount that goes to pay principal for 15- and 30-year loans. Notice the amount going to principal after 10 years. In the case of the shorter-term loan, the mortgage payback and equity increase is far higher.

It's true that the shorter-term mortgage appears to make better economic sense than the longer-term one. However, in most cases a shorter mortgage term will be the difference between negative and no-negative cashflow. That's all important.

As we've seen, having no negative cashflow should be our number one priority for a variety of reasons. After all, what good does mortgage payback and increased equity do us if we lose the property?

Furthermore, the way most modern mortgages are written, we can have our cake and eat it, too. Most mortgages today provide that the borrower can prepay the principal at any time. If that's the case, then *at our option* we can turn a 30-year mortgage into a 15-year mortgage by simply increasing the monthly payments by about 15 percent.

When we first buy the property, we may want the low payment benefit of the 30-year term. But after a few years, when we are able to raise rents and our break-even goes up, if we want to we can increase the amount we pay on the mortgage, pay it off much more quickly, and save a lot on interest.

The critical point is that with a 30-year mortgage *we* have the choice as to whether we'll make higher or lower payments. With a 15-year mortgage we have no option. We're locked in. Having that choice, to me, is worth paying the extra percent (or less) to get the longer term.

2.　Avoid Adjustable-Rate Mortgages

There are two exceptions to this, which I'll note in a moment. But first, let's be sure we understand the terminology. An *adjustable-rate mortgage* is one on which the interest rate can vary over the course of the mortgage. The other kind of mortgage is a *fixed-rate mortgage,* on which the interest rate remains constant for the life of the loan.

The problem with adjustable-rate mortgages is that when interest rates go up, so does the monthly payment. We could start out with a low monthly payment that enabled us to break even on the property. Then, interest rates in general could rise, triggering an increase in the interest rate on the mortgage, which would be reflected by a hike in the monthly payment. One month we could be at break-even; the next we could be suffering a substantial negative cashflow.

Some lenders suggest that they have moderated the problem by putting "caps," or limits, on the amount the interest rate can rise, the amount the monthly payment can rise, or both. I've examined literally dozens of different adjustable-rate mortgages, and my conclusion is that the lender's claims of success have been greatly exaggerated.

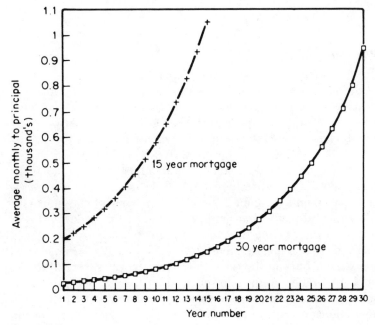

Figure 6.1

Most interest rate caps still allow a fluctuation of as much as 4 or 5 percent above the initial interest rate. Most mortgage payment caps still allow a higher monthly payment, just not high enough to take care of all the interest. So the interest that isn't paid monthly is added to the mortgage (negative amortization) and we end up paying interest on interest. The result is that the mortgage grows bigger instead of getting smaller, eating away at appreciation and equity.

Worst of all, the introductory interest rate on many (if not most) adjustable-rate mortgages is a teaser. It's a buy-down from the true rate. For example, if the true mortgage interest rate were 10 percent, to induce people to get the less desirable adjustable-rate mortgage, a teaser rate of 8 percent might be offered.

An investor getting this mortgage might think he or she had a good deal—until the first adjustment period, usually not more than 6 months later. At that time, the mortgage would begin moving up to the market rate of 10 percent. Thus, even if interest rates in general don't rise, with an adjustable-rate mortgage, the interest rate and monthly payments could still go up!

Generally speaking, adjustable-rate mortgages are a bad thing for the investor. Besides the specific problems we've noted, there's the uncertainty of them. Not knowing what the payment is going to be each month can be the worst problem of all.

When to Get an Adjustable-Rate Mortgage

I noted at the onset that there were two times when an adjustable-rate mortgage made sense for the investor. The first is when we plan on a quick turnover of the property (Game Plan 3). In that case, we don't care if the interest rate and the monthly payment are going to rise, because we won't be holding onto the property for long anyhow.

In this situation, the added advantage of an adjustable-rate mortgage is that frequently the costs are lower. When we obtain a mortgage we usually must pay points (1 point is equal to 1 percent of the mortgage amount). With an adjustable-rate mortgage, the points are often lower than with a fixed-rate, saving us some closing costs.

The other time to consider an adjustable-rate mortgage is when interest rates are very high. Back in the early 1980s, interest rates were in the 15 percent and higher range. At the same time, adjustable-rate mortgages were often offered at 2 to 3 percent below the cost of a fixed-rate mortgage.

The thing about interest rates is that, historically, they never *remain* high. They always seem eventually to come down. Therefore, when rates are high, getting an adjustable-rate mortgage may make sense *if* we plan to refinance within two years.

The process is to get the adjustable-rate mortgage upon buying the property, then refinance after no more than two years (when rates, hopefully, are lower), and then get a fixed-rate mortgage. Of course, there will be the additional costs of the refinancing, but we should figure that as part of our initial investment when we buy the property.

3. Look for Existing Low-Interest-Rate FHA/VA Loans

What makes government-insured (FHA) or guaranteed (VA) loans so appealing is that they are assumable. Conventional (any nongovernment) loans generally are not.

If we can find a property with an FHA/VA loan on it, we can assume that loan *without any qualifying* (see the FHA exception below) and we won't have to pay the costs (often 5 percent of the loan amount) of getting new financing. In addition, when it comes time to sell, the next buyer can assume the loan from us. (Recently, the FHA has been requiring a good credit report before allowing buyers to assume existing FHA loans.)

FHA/VA loans are good deals for investors—provided they are at the right interest rate.

The problem with many of these loans is that they were issued in the period between 1980 and 1984 when interest rates were relatively high. Thus, although the market rate at the time we are buying a property may be 9 percent, an FHA or VA existing loan may be 13 percent. Is it a good deal now?

From the perspective of avoiding negative cashflow, probably not. The 3 or 4 percent difference in interest is sure to make a substantial difference in our monthly payment. If we get a mortgage at the new market rate, we might be able to break even or better. But getting the older FHA or VA loan may make the payments so high that we can't come out ahead.

Thus, getting an FHA/VA loan is a good idea *only* if we can get it at a good interest rate.

Beware FHA/VA Loan Scams

Some schemers, seeing the value of government loans, have taken advantage of the situation. They have created scams that are currently being investigated by various branches of the federal government.

The scams work like this. A schemer comes into town and, either through advertising, hunting through for-sale properties, or contacting brokers and lenders, locates all the FHA/VA properties for sale. He or she then makes "nothing down" offers on all of them!

(As noted in an earlier chapter, the nothing-down offer consists of deferring the down payment into the future. For example, instead of coming up with cash down, this schemer gives the seller a second mortgage for the whole down payment, due and payable in 3 years with interest, but with *no monthly payments*. Since the government mortgages are assumable, there's virtually no qualifying and the sale is quickly consummated.)

Once the schemer gains control of the property, he or she rents it out and never makes another mortgage payment.

The foreclosure process with government loans is often quite lengthy. As a result, it often takes anywhere from 5 months to 2 years before foreclosure occurs. During that time, the schemer is collecting rents and not making payments.

Ultimately the lender forecloses. When this happens, the seller finds out that the second mortgage for the down payment is going to become worthless. To save the equity in the property, the former owner must now foreclose on the second mortgage and make up all the back payments on the government first mortgage. By the time the seller is done, he or she has paid out many months of mortgage payments and has accumulated attorney's fees plus the original closing costs (usually including a broker's commission) that were paid up front when the sale was made! In the meantime, the schemer pockets many months of rent and leaves town.

How does this scam affect an investor? Obviously, for a seller, it's something to watch out for. However, it's also a problem for a buyer. Today, sellers, brokers, lenders, virtually anyone involved in the industry is on the alert for these schemers and this scam. Therefore, anyone trying to buy a property with an FHA/VA loan is immediately going to be suspect, even if they've done nothing wrong.

That translates into a harder time convincing the seller to sell, which could necessitate putting up more cash as the down payment.

The bottom line here is that FHA/VA loans with low interest rates are a good deal. But be prepared for a hassle when you try to get one.

4. Use Lines of Credit for Quick Deals

This is an idea that relatively few investors use, which is a shame. It takes courage, quickness, and foresight. But it can offer big payoffs in reduced closing costs, lower purchase prices, and deals made that would otherwise slip through our fingers.

The concept is simply that, instead of buying a property with a mortgage, which is the accepted practice, we buy it for all cash. All cash is a tremendous bargaining point. It means we can close quickly. Most real estate transactions take 4 to 8 weeks to close, primarily because the buyer must qualify for a mortgage. But, if we come in offering all cash, we eliminate that lengthy escrow period. To sellers who want to get out of their properties right away, it can mean making a deal. To the investor who uses it, it can mean getting a better price.

The catch, of course, is that most of us just don't have the cash to do this kind of deal—or do we?

What does "all cash" mean in a real estate transaction? It means that the full purchase price is paid in cash. It means the seller gets his or her money out and the existing mortgage(s) is paid off.

Does it mean that the buyer must put in all the cash? Not necessarily. Of course the buyer could. But the buyer doesn't have to, as long as there is enough cash from some source to close escrow. To put it another way, if the buyer can borrow the needed cash in a short enough time *without getting a mortgage on the property,* then it's the same as all cash as far as the seller is concerned. (That's where the courage comes in.)

Making this technique work, therefore, comes down to being able to borrow enough to close the deal without using a mortgage on the property. Typically, that means borrowing about $100,000 or more.

You say you couldn't possibly do that? Have you tried?

Sources of Cash Financing

One enterprising young woman I met accomplished this just through the use of credit cards. Her credit rating was good. And she was constantly besieged by banks from all over the country offering her VISA or MasterCard credit lines worth between $3000 and $5000. She accepted them all.

Yes, she paid quite a few annual fees. But by the time she had two dozen or so cards, she had the equivalent of $100,000 in credit available. She never borrowed against the cards—until she decided to buy a property. Then she used the lines of credit in cash, from each account. When she went to buy property, she paid cash! And she got the commensurate benefits of a very low price.

Daring? Yes it was. But not as daring as it at first seemed. After all, once she had the property she could quickly go out and secure a new first mortgage. She then could pay back the card debt and be out, at the most, the interest for a month or two on the credit cards.

Or, and this was her primary plan (Game Plan 3), she could quickly resell. Remember, by paying cash she avoided most closing costs associated with mortgages. She bought low by using cash, then resold for the normal market price. She netted an average of about $10,000 on each property.

There are, of course, hidden risks. There is no guarantee that any lender will offer a mortgage on a given piece of property. There could be a problem with the house or the title. There could be termite infestation requiring costly repair. Any number of unforseen things could occur. But she was gutsy and she took the chance. The last I saw of her she was still doing about three houses a year this way.

Some feel that using credit cards is a crude (but effective) way of establishing lines of credit. A more direct approach is simply to make friends with a banker and then ask directly for a big line of credit. If you have a good credit history, have other collateral (such as the house in which you live), and have some history of business success, you will probably get it. If one bank won't give you a big enough credit line, talk to three or four banks and get several.

5. Negotiate a Second with a Lower Monthly Payment

Very frequently, the seller will carry back some of the financing on a purchase. The terms of this seller financing are totally negotiable and often can be arranged to help a buyer come out with no negative cash-flow.

Of all sellers, 95 percent are hung up on price. If we give them the price they want, they are often more than willing to accept less favorable (to them) terms on the financing. Let's assume that we're purchasing a property for $100,000. We're assuming an existing VA loan for $50,000, and the seller is giving us a new second mortgage for $40,000.

The terms of the VA mortgage are fixed and leave us no room for change. But the terms of the second are not. We can arrange any terms agreeable to both buyer and seller. Here are two ways the terms of a second mortgage could be arranged. (Assume a market interest rate of 10 percent.)

Negotiating for Terms of the Second

Factors	Favorable to seller	Favorable to buyer
Amount	$40,000	$40,000
Interest rate	12%	8%
Term	5 years	15 years
Fully amortized monthly payment	$890	$383
Interest-only monthly payment	400	267

Notice the vastly reduced monthly payment *if* we make the terms of the second more favorable to the buyer. (Lowering the interest rate more would decrease the monthly payments even further.) How likely is a seller to accept the less favorable terms? My experience has been that, as long as sellers get full price, they will often accept outrageous terms, such as a 6 percent interest rate when the market rate is 10 percent.

Note, however, that there could be a tax problem here *for the seller.* The government may impute a market rate even when one isn't given. For example, interest received is generally taxable. In the less favorable deal just illustrated, the seller was given an 8 percent mortgage when the market rate was 10 percent. The seller would want to declare and pay interest on 8 percent. But the government may impute a market rate and insist the seller pay taxes on the full 10 percent, even though he or she didn't receive that high a rate!

Negotiating for an interest-only loan (balloon payment) will also lower the monthly payment. However, remember that on an interest-only loan, at the end of the term, the full amount of the mortgage comes due. Therefore, getting a long term is essential here.

Negotiating with the seller for more favorable terms of a second mortgage is an excellent way of reducing the monthly payment and, thereby, goes a long way to creating a no-negative property.

6. Buy Back a Second at Discount

Here is another seller financing technique that requires a certain amount of courage but offers big payoffs if it works.

In this case, the buyer gives the seller a substantial second mortgage for most of the down payment. Then the buyer buys that second back from the seller for cash at a hefty discount. In the course of the transaction, the buyer, in effect, gets the property for a reduced price. Here's an exaggerated example to show how it works:

A seller has a property for which he is asking $100,000. Our buyer likes the property. However, if she pays $100,000 ($20,000 down and gets a new $80,000 mortgage), her monthly payments will be $150 a month higher than her projected rental income. The property will have a negative cashflow and, therefore, not be a worthwhile investment.

However, our buyer is creative. She discovers that the seller has an existing $50,000 FHA *assumable* mortgage. She also knows the seller needs *cash*. So she makes him this *offer on a $100,000 house:*

Cash down	$ 10,000
Second mortgage	40,000
FHA first	+50,000
Purchase price	$100,000

The seller is induced to take the offer because it is full price. It goes to escrow.

Either in escrow or shortly after the deal closes (this is the part that takes courage, because the seller might not accept), the buyer offers to "cash out" the second mortgage. She will give the seller the discounted cash value of the mortgage. She offers 60 percent. (Second mortgages are cashed out not for full value, but for a discount based on their *present* value. The discount depends on how the mortgage was written, the interest rate, the term, and the market conditions at the time. Typical discounts range from 50 to 80 percent.)

Because the seller wants cash, he agrees. The buyer gives him 60 percent of the $40,000 note, or $24,000 in cash. [She obtains this money by getting a "hard money" (all cash) second for 15 years from a local savings and loan.]

The following illustrates how the deal looks *after paying off the discounted second:*

Cash down	$10,000
New second	24,000
FHA first	+50,000
Effective purchase price	$84,000

The house that had a negative cashflow at a $100,000 purchase price ends up with at least a break-even at an $84,000 purchase price.

Why It Works

There are several critical issues to understand here. First, the seller must be willing to sell the second mortgage at a discount. A seller who holds the mortgage to term will receive the full payoff. If our buyer has wrongly judged the seller, she could stand to lose.

Seconds may be discounted during escrow. That is, the seller who wants cash badly enough may be willing to discount the second even before the deal closes. This is the ideal case for the buyer, who then takes little risk (since the tricky part is getting the second discounted occurs after the deal closes).

A seller, however, may be resistant to discounting a second *to a buyer*. The attitude, in this case, may be, "She's actually offering me $16,000 less than sales price!" This is of course true. However, it may be the case that the property is actually worth $16,000 less, but the seller is hung up on price. Discounting a second is often a method of showing a seller the true value of his or her property.

As previously mentioned, the amount of discount of the second depends on how it is written. (Terms of second mortgages given by sellers are always negotiable.) Here are the items that increase the value of a second. Leaving them out or lowering them, on the other hand, lowers the second mortgage's value.

The following factors *increase* the value of a second mortgage:

Interest rate at or higher than market

Penalty for late monthly payment

Short term

Full amortization (no balloon)

High equity in property

The following factors *decrease* the value of a second mortgage:

Interest rate below market

No penalty for late monthly payment

Long term

Big balloon payment

Questionable equity in property to back up second

The buyer must have cash to buy out the second. In our example, the buyer went to a local savings and loan and got a replacement second. These days, most S & Ls will offer cash seconds for close-to-market interest rates, fully amortized for terms of up to 15 years. These seconds are almost as good as some firsts.

On the other hand, our buyer could have completely refinanced. She could have gotten a new first to pay off both the existing FHA loan *and* the discounted second. The question would be, could she have gotten a large enough first to accomplish this?

Existing first	$50,000
Discounted second	+24,000
New first needed	$74,000

In the illustration, her new first just equalled the payoffs of the old first and second. If she had gotten more money on a new first, however, she could have paid off costs plus perhaps even gotten some of her original down payment back. In our example, however, the buyer elected to go for a new second because she wanted to keep the existing FHA loan with its assumability advantage (for when she wanted to resell).

7. Give an Interest in Other Property or Other Collateral

Yet another way of reducing monthly payments is to give an interest in other property or give other collateral. This works quite simply.

Most of us are locked into thinking of using the subject property as the sole collateral for financing. We have heard that we can get 80 or 90 percent of the value of the property as a mortgage and so on. But, what we tend to overlook is that we can often finance the purchase of one property with another.

For example, we want to buy a $100,000 property. The seller once again has an assumable $50,000 first, and we are putting $10,000 cash down. However, if we give the seller a $40,000 second with $400-a-month payments, we will end up with a $100-a-month negative cashflow. (Our expenses, including mortgage, will exceed potential rental income by $100 monthly.)

What if, however, we *only* had the $50,000 first on the property and no second? Instead of a $100 monthly negative cashflow, we would have a $300 positive cashflow. Sounds great, right? But what happens to that $40,000 second that we don't give the seller on the property?

If we own other property, we can instead give the seller an interest in that. For example, let's say that we own a duplex in which we have $50,000 equity. We now make the seller the following *collateralized offer:*

Down payment	$ 10,000
Assume existing FHA loan	50,000
Interest in duplex	+40,000
Total	$100,000

If the seller accepts, we end up with a property in which we have a $50,000 equity having put only $10,000 down. Additionally, since we have no second mortgage, we end up with a positive cashflow of $300 monthly!

Why would a seller do this?

The seller may want out badly. (Maybe it's already a rental property and the seller doesn't want the headache.) He or she may be induced by the $10,000 cash we are putting down. It really makes no difference why the seller would accept, chances are that out of every ten offers made like this, one or two sellers would accept. After all, assuming the duplex does have $50,000 in equity, the offer is very strong. There is no hanky-panky, and it's a chance for the seller to get out of the property.

Structuring the Collateral

For the buyer this is a very sweet deal. On the subject property, obviously there is the positive cashflow plus the big equity. However, on the collateral property (duplex), there is also a big plus. The seller may give up a $40,000 interest in the property *without giving up the right to the cashflow.*

There are many ways of handling this. The seller of the subject property could be made a tenant-in-common on the deed and given a specific interest in the property. Or he or she could be given a note and trust deed for $40,000, no interest, due and payable in 3 to 5 years when the property is sold.

The idea, however, is that the seller of the subject property receives as part of the down payment equity in another property instead of cash. And that equity is not interest-bearing.

Thus, if the buyer were, for example, receiving a $300 monthly cashflow on the duplex, he or she would continue to receive that income plus the $300 monthly on the subject property. And when the duplex was sold, the buyer of the subject property would be entitled to the

$10,000 equity that remained at the time of the transaction *plus* all or part of any appreciation which occurred subsequently.

Using equity in another property is, in the country today, one of the fastest-growing means of pyramiding real estate. It's quick and it's profitable. The key to it is, of course, to have equity in another property *and* to keep your eye on the cashflow.

Other Collateral

Of course, thus far we've been assuming that the collateral was in the form of another property. The reason is that collateralizing other real estate is the easiest to understand for most sellers. However, anything in which we own equity will do. I have seen buyers use motor homes and boats as collateral. It's not beyond reason that autos, furniture, jewelry, or even motorcycles could be used—if, in fact, the equity did exist in them.

The point is that this method, though seldom used, allows for almost endless improvisation. For example, this is one of the few methods that legitimately allows you to buy properties for nothing down *with* positive cashflow. (You just offer as the down payment equity only in something else. Of course, sellers are far more reluctant to accept an offer that has little or no cash in it than one in which the buyer is putting some cash down.) All that it requires is that you start off with some equity in something. After that, it's all a matter of finding willing sellers and of parlaying what you have into something really exciting.

It should be noted that this method of pyramiding is not new or even unusual. It is commonly done by giant corporations and large real estate investment organizations to increase their holdings.

8. Put More Cash Down

This is sure to make most readers squirm. However, if you want to achieve a significant cashflow, the most secure way of doing it is to put more money down. This is essentially what was discussed under "Game Plan 2."

Many older Americans have accumulated substantial amounts of capital over the years. Their choice is to put it in "paper" investments, such as stocks, bonds, or CDs, or to stick it into physical investments, such as real estate. The latter, upon consideration, has a great deal to offer. The following is an example:

Sally is a widow looking for an apartment in which to live. She has $200,000 in cash to invest and she wants both income and security for the money. But she needs at least $1000 a month on which to live. She is considering the purchase of a small apartment building. It has eight units rented out for $500 monthly apiece, or $4000 total, $48,000 annually. The asking price is $300,000. (We'll go into how the asking price is determined in a later chapter on apartment and office buildings.)

Sally likes the apartment building, because she can get a positive cashflow and can live in one of the units. Here's how the deal works out:

Sally's Apartment Building

Down payment	$200,000	
Mortgage	+100,000	
Purchase price	$300,000	
Total monthly income		
(less one unit Sally lives in)		$3500
Monthly expenses		
Mortgage (10 % for 30 years)	$ 878	
Taxes	375	
Insurance	100	
Maintenance, management, and upkeep	+800	
Total monthly expenses	$2153	−2153
Positive cashflow		$1347

By putting a substantial amount of money into the property, Sally accomplished at least three of her objectives:

1. She has a place to live.
2. She has invested her money at a good return. (Not counting appreciation or her free apartment, her money is receiving about 6.8 percent. If the apartment is counted, her return is actually over 9 percent.)
3. She has over $1000 in cash each month on which to live.

In addition, she is receiving the added benefit of future appreciation. Assuming the apartment building goes up in value, her original $200,000 investment will grow each year.

Finally, since the property is her total income, she can use depreciation (as well as deductions for interest, taxes, and other costs) to help offset her gain on that portion of the property in which she does not live (⅞) and, as a result, most of the income she gets is not immediately taxable, i.e., deferred into the future. Since Sally is already well past her 60s, she isn't really worried about any eventual gain. (It's something her heirs will have to consider, though!)

Putting a lot of money down on real estate, typically about 50 percent, can produce a significant positive cashflow. If you have cash and what you want is a positive cashflow as well as a good investment, it's something to consider.

These eight techniques and tips should go a long way toward helping you get started in finding real estate with no negative. But don't think they are the only ones. In real estate financing, we are limited only by our imaginations.

7

The Real Truth About Ownership Costs

I was recently watching TV when a likeable-looking fellow came on to explain how to make a million dollars in real estate working weekends and holidays. Some of the person's suggestions, actually, were quite good. But where I found a real stumbling block was in his description of property ownership. He made a list of costs that looked like this:

Mortgage payment

Taxes

Insurance

These he added up and explained as the expenses. They then were subtracted from the monthly income to show a positive cashflow.

I am absolutely convinced that many reasonable people watching the show saw nothing wrong with this. At the same time, I'm quite sure anyone experienced in real estate was guffawing. For the truth was that our TV guru had left out some very important and costly expenses of ownership.

Perhaps he wasn't concerned about these because, as he pointed out, he only planned on holding the property for six months or less. Then he would sell for a whopping big profit. But realistically in today's market, that just may not be possible. Holding for five or more years may be necessary before reaping a profit. During that time, what if the true expenses had been grossly underestimated?

The Real Costs

In this chapter, we are going to look more realistically at the costs of real estate ownership. They will have an enormous impact on cashflow. But before you read on, please understand that this is a no-holds-barred approach. If you're faint of heart, don't continue.

Ownership Costs

The only honest way to calculate ownership costs is over a long period of time. For example, over its lifetime, any property will require maintenance and repairs. But in any given year, while it might not require a dollar to be spent, it might need thousands of dollars of repair work. (Funny how that TV guru happened always to pick the year that no work was required!)

If we hold property over a period of time, however, we can expect all typical costs to catch up with us and to average out. Therefore, for this chapter we are going to assume that we hold property for 10 years. We might end up holding it for only 5 or 3 years, but that shouldn't make any difference. We'll calculate the total costs for 10 years and then come up with an average yearly cost.

The property in question is a small (1500-square-foot) single-family residence (see Table 7.1). We're renting it out ourselves (not using a management company). We'll assign a typical lifespan for each item found in the home. (Remember, we're talking about rental property, where tenants don't usually give equipment loving, tender care. Consequently, the lifespan may be shorter than a similar item would be in your own home.)

Table 7.1 Costs of Ownership by Item, Life, and Cost (1987 Prices)

Item	Lifespan, years	Replacement cost, dollars	Average annual cost, dollars
Water heater	7	300	43
Dishwasher	5	300	60
Garbage disposal	4	100	25
Stove/oven	10	500	50
Washers/faucets	1	25	50
(per instance, 2 per year)			
Carpeting	5	2400	480
(120 yards @ $20 per yard)			
Paint interior	2	750	375
Paint exterior	6	750	125
Clean-up (after tenants leave and before rerenting)	1	500	500

Table 7.1 Costs of Ownership by Item, Life, and Cost (1987 Prices) (*Continued*)

Item	Lifespan, years	Replacement cost, dollars	Average annual cost, dollars
Advertising	1	25	25
Yard care	1	75	75
(including fertilizer, but not mowing or gardening)			
Miscellaneous	1	100	100
(including breakage of windows, screens, etc.)			
Total annualized costs of ownership			1908
Monthly			159
Air Conditioning (optional):			
Compressor	10	700	70
Upkeep	1	75	75
Total annualized with air conditioning			2053
Monthly			171
Pool (optional):			
Pump and filter replacement	7	1000	143
Chemicals	1	300	25
Cleaning	1	300	25
Total annualized with pool			2246
Monthly			187

What Table 7.1 illustrates is that the actual, true costs of ownership over a 10-year period for a modest-sized, 1500-square-foot rental house will average about $160 a month. (With air conditioning it goes up to $171 per month. With air conditioning and a pool, it's $187 per month.)

How to Use These Costs

The costs just described are *in addition* to the costs normally given for owning rental property. They are in addition to:

Mortgage payment (principal and interest)

Taxes

Insurance

(*Note:* Insurance will be higher if your rental property has a pool. You will need to carry substantially higher liability coverage to protect yourself in the event of an accident.)

In addition, no cost was listed for management. This includes answering phone calls from tenants with problems; placing ads in papers and "For Rent" signs on the property; showing the property; and doing odd repair, clean-up, and maintenance jobs. If you have a property management company handle the property for you, as a rule you can just about double the costs given.

When you buy a rental property, unless you plan a quick turnover (Game Plan 3), you *must* include these costs if you want a realistic estimate of your expenses. Anytime you don't add in at least the minimum figure, you are not getting an honest estimate.

It Won't Happen to Me

Having thus described the real costs of maintenance, I would be remiss if I didn't mention those who feel somehow immune from them. I know that there are a certain number of readers who are saying to themselves, "Pooh. Those are 10-year average costs. If I buy and hold the property for only 2 or 3 years and am *just a little bit lucky,* I can get away without any of those costs. And it wouldn't take that much. If during my short ownership I don't have to replace carpeting, water heater, compressor, or other appliances, those costs go down to nothing. I'll figure $25 a month and chances are I'll get away with it!"

The argument is both true and false. It's true in that, if you own the property a short time and are lucky, you may have only minor repair and maintenance costs.

It's false for two reasons. The first is that, since the Tax Reform Act, we are mostly looking to long-term ownership of real estate. Over the long-term, the costs will get you. The second is that, while you may be lucky and have no major repairs over 2 to 3 years, you could be unlucky and have lots of major repairs during that time. The compressor, carpeting, water heater, and other items could all need to be replaced in the first year! With short-term ownership, you'd have only 2 to 3 years instead of 10 over which to capitalize those expenses. Your actual out-of-pocket costs, in this case, could be 2 to 3 times the estimates given here!

Other Problems

Proper maintenance does not take into account other potential problems that could occur. These include vacancies and problem tenants.

As an owner of property, we have to find the right tenants. As we all know, the right tenant is one who pays the rent, who doesn't make a mess, and who doesn't complain too much. As long as the tenant fits these three criteria, we're likely to be satisfied.

However, it may occasionally happen that we rent to a tenant who does the three worst things that can happen to any rental:

1. The tenant damages the property.
2. The tenant does not pay the rent.
3. Worst of all, the tenant does not move out.

Usually all three go together.

When this happens, and it will happen to you if you have enough rentals and rent long enough, it's going to be costly.

Eviction

If a tenant damages the property but still pays the rent, we can ask the tenant to leave. Most month-to-month rental agreements contain a clause that states that, for whatever reason, either tenant or landlord can terminate the agreement within 30 days. Most leases contain a clause that states that damage to the property by the tenant is sufficient reason for breaking the lease.

The tenant who leaves when asked, even though the property is damaged, does not usually hurt the landlord very much. Usually, most of the damage can be paid for out of the security deposit.

The real problems occur, however, when, besides damage, the tenant refuses to pay the rent and does not leave.

Years ago, many parts of the country had something called "self-help evictions." If the tenant didn't pay the rent and wouldn't leave, we could hire some burly fellows, go in, and bodily throw the person and his or her furniture out. Those days, however, are long gone. Today, removing a tenant even for just cause requires legal action.

It requires first that a formal, written notice be sent to the tenant stating that, if rent is not paid (usually in 3 days), eviction proceedings will be started. If the tenant still doesn't pay, you must file a "writ of unlawful detainer." In most locales, an attorney is not required to file it. However, until you've done it once or twice, you will need an attorney to do it for you. The time it takes to get an unlawful detainer action often depends on how much rent we are charging. Depending on the jurisdiction, the amount of rent will determine whether it goes before municipal court (lower rent) or superior court (higher rent). Generally, if it goes to superior court, it takes longer, is more complex, and costs more.

Additionally, eviction doesn't happen immediately. Almost no judge will act until the tenant is at least two weeks behind in rent. Then, if and when the judge does act, it may take another week or two to get the actual eviction. From the time it is started, a normal eviction proceeding takes at least a full month.

Finally, if eviction is necessary, it's normally handled by the sheriff or other appropriate law enforcement agency. The sheriff comes in and, if necessary, bodily removes the tenant. (If the tenant happens to be pregnant or seriously ill, eviction may be stayed—without rent paid—for many, many months. Fortunately, this rarely happens.)

Then the sheriff's helpers (for whom we have to pay) take all the tenant's possessions and put them in storage for a proscribed period of time. We also have to pay for the moving and storage. Eventually the items are sold at public auction (for which we pay). However, any money received will normally be returned to us to help defray costs. (Unfortunately, tenants who have to be evicted rarely have anything worth much, and the auctions usually don't bring in much money.)

Above all, while this is going on, the property is not bringing in any rental income. As a result, tenants who damage the property, don't pay rent, and won't move are exceedingly costly. If, for example, we were renting property in California for over $1000 monthly and had to evict, here are some *typical eviction costs we might have to pay*:

Court costs	$200
Attorney fees	450
Bond (for movers)	150
Sheriff and other costs	100
Document filing and other fees	+100
	$1000
Lost rent (1 month)	1000
Extra repairs	+1000
Total costs	$3000

Of course, the above figures do not take into account the normal costs of cleaning after a tenant leaves, the month we may have waited before filing for eviction hoping the tenant would pay, or the costs of rerenting.

Placing the Costs

Where do we add in the costs for possible eviction? It's really hard to do. Many landlords after years of renting never have to evict anyone. Others may have two or three evictions in a single year.

My own feeling is that evictions are a hidden cost. We can't really calculate them on an average yearly basis because they may very well not happen to us. We can only be aware of the potential and stand ready in case they do become a reality.

Good Management

It's been said before but bears repeating. The best way to avoid evictions is not to rent to bad tenants. Renting to good tenants will help ensure that we don't have to pay eviction costs.

Unfortunately, there's no sure-fire method of doing this. However, there are some precautions that normally can be taken. For example:

1. Have the tenants fill out a questionnaire before signing a lease or rental agreement. It's important that the tenant agrees to allow you to check credit and verify statements on the report. (A typical questionnaire, Figure 7.1, is illustrated at the end of this section. Use it as a guide.)

2. Always get a credit report on prospective tenants.

3. Verify employment and bank accounts.

4. *Check with former landlords.* If you do nothing else, this *must* be done. It is the quickest, cheapest, and easiest way to determine the kind of tenant you may be getting. I know landlords who, as a rule, refuse to rent to any tenant who does not provide the name and phone number of his or her previous two landlords.

Finally, it all comes down to judging character. I have broken all the rules when it comes to renting. I have rented to college students (something that many landlords advise against because of their tendency to have parties and to be transient); I have rented to individuals who literally had no credit and no bank account but paid cash; I have rented to groups of individuals who got together to share a house. Rarely has it gotten me into trouble. Talk to your next tenants, get to know and understand them, get a feeling for the kind of people they are. That can be your best assurance of finding the right people.

```
NAME OF ALL ADULTS TO OCCUPY PROPERTY
NAME OF ALL OTHER OCCUPANTS (Children)
NUMBER AND TYPE OF PETS
CURRENT ADDRESS
    Landlord's name and phone number
REASON FOR LEAVING
PREVIOUS ADDRESS
    Landlord's name and phone number
EMPLOYED BY
    Immediate supervisor and phone number
    Salary or income
OTHER OCCUPANT EMPLOYED BY
    Immediate supervisor and phone number
    Salary or income
BIRTH DATE(S) (All tenants)
CREDIT CARD ISSUER(S) AND NUMBER(S) (List 2)
SOCIAL SECURITY NUMBER(S)
DRIVER'S LICENSE NUMBER(S)
NAME(S) OF BANK AND ACCOUNT
AUTO LICENSE NUMBER(S)
    State of registry
    Make and model
WHOM TO CALL IN AN EMERGENCY
```

Figure 7.1

Note: The tenant must be willing to volunteer this information. In addition, the tenant must sign a statement authorizing the landlord or his or her agent to verify the information, including a credit report. If the tenant does not authorize it, the landlord probably has no right to make such inquiries and could be liable to the prospective tenant for invasion of privacy.

The Importance of Accurate Estimates

In the old days of capital gains and tax shelters, being off on the expenses was a minor problem. Any additional expenses just added to the write-off. In effect, Uncle Sam made up part of our mistake.

But today, we pay the full cost ourselves. In a small property, knowing that maintenance and repair costs can average $160 or more a month can make a big difference. Knowing that a month or two's worth of rent (not to mention other costs) can be lost due to bad tenants can also make a significant difference. These added expenses can mean the difference between a positive and a negative cashflow. They can also mean that properties which at first seemed acceptable, really aren't.

8
Raising Rents

We have thus far been examining the expense side of property owner-ship. Now it's time to look at the other side of the ledger—income. Just as there are hidden costs, tricks, and stumbling blocks in expenses that can cause us to have negative cashflow, so too are there items that cause us not to get our best possible rent. In this chapter, we'll look more closely at these.

The Importance of Rent

Obviously rent is important. Most of us count on it to offset expenses. Relatively few people buy property with the intention of just letting it sit without producing any income and paying for it out of pocket (vacation property is an exception).

The more rent we receive, the more likely we are to show a positive cashflow. The real question becomes, therefore, what is the most effec-tive way of getting the highest possible rent for a piece of property?

Getting the Highest Rent

In this chapter, we're going to assume that we are renting either a single-family residence, a condo, or a very small apartment building (less than four units). The reason we're not going to consider bigger residential rentals is simple: In most areas of the country, individual units or small apartment buildings normally do not fall under any form of rent con-trol. Bigger units do.

Raising rents under rent control is strictly supervised and, hence, there's not much flexibility for the landlord. On the other hand, in non-rent-controlled property, rents are limited only by market conditions and the landlord's creativity.

The examples we are going to look at and the rules we are going to give, therefore, apply to a non–rent-controlled market. We are going to see what conditions determine the maximum rent and what we, as landlords, can do to change them.

What, then, is the highest rent that we can get for our property? In an earlier chapter we looked at ways to determine in advance what the true rent was likely to be. Once we obtain our property, however, all previous estimates fly out the window. Now it's do or die. We will very quickly find out the amount for which we can (and can't) rent a property. Therefore, as a second assumption, we are going to be renting out a property that we just bought. We haven't rented it before, hence, we have no previous rental experience on which to rely with this particular house.

The Property

We have bought a nice three-bedroom, two-bath house in a reasonably desirable neighborhood. Our previous analysis told us that rents in the area were in the $800 to $1000 range. Our break-even is $900 a month. The property closed yesterday and today's our first day of possession. Where do we go from here?

Finding Tenants

There are many ways of finding tenants, including checking with, and putting our name on lists at, large companies and institutions (such as colleges) that have housing offices; listing our property with brokers; putting up bulletins at supermarkets; and so forth.

However, in our case we are going to use two tried-and-true methods—a sign on the front of the property and an ad in the paper. We are going to use these because we are waging war against a trying enemy—time. Time is against us.

If our break-even is $900 a month, each day that goes by during which our property is not rented costs us $30 out of pocket. If we waste just one week looking for a tenant, it will cost us $210. At those prices, we simply can't afford to hesitate. We must find a tenant, and right away.

Some experienced landlords have a clause right in the purchase agreement that allows them to show the property *before* the deal closes. These investors show and try to rent the house even before they buy it. That way, the day the deal closes, they can have a tenant ready to move in and no time at all is lost.

The Best Source

Ask any experienced landlord around the country—the most effective way of locating a tenant is through an ad in the local newspaper. That's where prospective tenants look when they want to rent. That's where we must tell them that we have a house available.

The other excellent place to find tenants is simply to put a large "For Rent" sign in the front of the property. Prospective renters may be hunting the area for a home to rent. They may be looking for our house. But they won't find it unless we tell them it's there. That's what the sign does.

The Ad Itself

Aware of the need to find tenants quickly, some owners, particularly those new to the business, take out a big newspaper ad listing the various features of the property. It's easy to fill twenty or thirty lines, going on about how wonderful is the carpeting, the yard, the view, or whatever else we have to offer.

Big advertisements are unnecessary, expensive, and sometimes counterproductive. When it comes to finding a place to rent from an ad, most tenants are looking for the three basics: location, size, and price. If the unit fits those criteria, chances are the prospective tenant will come by to see if they like everything else. Consequently, all we really need to get across are the basics.

Having rented property more times than I care to remember, I don't believe I've ever run an ad that was more than three lines long. I always try to cover the basics plus any special amenities that might induce a tenant to check out the property. Here, for example is an actual ad that I ran not long ago:

LOVELY POOL HOME

Lg. 3+2, fireplace, good location.
Clean. $1,000 Phone ####

Not much to it. But it did tell prospective tenants that the home had a pool, it was large, it had three bedrooms and two baths (and a fireplace). Instead of listing the address, I instead put "good location." The reason was simple. The ad went into a small local paper with a circulation limited to the suburb in which the house was located. Those reading this paper already knew the general location. I wanted them to call me to find out the specific address. (My reasoning was that I wanted an opportunity to question prospective tenants a bit before sending them out to a vacant property. I didn't want any vandals calling up and then breaking in and ruining the house.)

The ad got results. I received no less than four phone calls a day and rented the home within 3 days. It's a true story.

The Starting Rental Rate

The single most important item in the ad is the rental rate. We are in competition with other landlords. Tenants have a maximum rent they are prepared to pay. If our ad offers at least as much as any other landlord for about the same price, we'll get calls. On the other hand, if our ad is for $1500 when there are dozens (if not hundreds) of other properties going for $1000, we shouldn't expect too many calls.

Tenants are rate-sensitive. Our rental rate needs to be right to get them at least to call to find out what we have to offer.

Earlier in the book, I suggested starting with a rate that was substantially higher than the analysis showed the market to be, then working down. That's a good idea. As regards the property in the ad shown, I had already tested the water and knew exactly what the market might bring. But in our example, we have just bought our test house and we don't yet know the market.

Our analysis showed that the rental range was from $800 to $1000. Now we have a choice to make. Do we want to rent as quickly as possible or as high as possible?

If we want to rent as quickly as possible, then we should start by advertising the property at $900 a month, our break-even. Hopefully that will bring in lots of calls.

On the other hand, if we're willing to sacrifice some rent to get a higher rental rate (remember, it costs us $30 a day to keep the place empty), we can try a higher rate. In this situation, I would try $1050. That's $50 higher than the top of the market, according to our market analysis. I would be willing to sacrifice several week's rent to see if I couldn't get better than market.

The way to work it is to try it for *one week*. If we rent it, we can congratulate ourselves. If we get a lot of calls, get prospective tenants who are willing to pay the price but just don't want our place for other reasons, we can try it for another week.

But, if we don't get calls or if the calls we get turn out to be from people who really don't want to rent the property at that price, then we should immediately drop our asking price by at least $50. We should try renting for $1000.

The same rules apply. Congratulations if we rent it. Try again if we come close. Drop it another $50 if there's poor or no response.

We work our way down, dropping the rent in decrements of $50 to the $900 break-even until we finally find tenants. We could, of course, end up losing several weeks rent this way. On the other hand, since we really don't know the market rate until we try, this helps us to feel confident that we are renting the property for the most we could hope to get.

When We Can't Rent for Break-Even

We keep lowering our rent until we reach $900 and we still can't find a tenant. What do we do? Do we just stick here and wait it out?

No, we keep dropping our rent even below the break-even to be assured that we get a tenant as quickly as possible. Who knows, we may have been totally wrong about rental rates in the area. We may not be able to rent until we drop the rate down to $800 a month.

Why Charge Less Than Break-Even

I'm sure many readers are wondering about asking a rental rate that's below break-even. In our example, renting for $800 monthly means we have a monthly negative of $100. Does that make sense?

The answer is simple. Let's say we are stubborn and insist on getting $900 a month and it takes us 7 weeks to find a suitable tenant. During those 7 weeks, we have lost 49 days rent, or $1633. On the other hand, let's say we are able to rent the property immediately at $800 a month. At the lower figure, it will take us more than 16 months to lose the same amount that we lost up front by waiting the extra 7 weeks to rent at a higher rate. With any luck, however, before those 16 months are up, we will be able to raise rents to our tenant, perhaps the full $100. Also, during that time, we may want to sell the property to avoid further losses.

It's always best to admit as soon as possible a mistake with regard to rental rates and to rent the property for whatever it will make. Keeping a property vacant for long periods of time while trying to get an unrealistic rent is a sure-fire way to the poorhouse.

Of course, with any luck we won't have to worry about break-even. In short order, we'll be able to rent for break-even or higher and start developing a positive cashflow.

Cleanliness

Thus far, we've dealt only with the basic house and the market. However, within any market, if we take all the houses that have the same basics (size, location, and rent), there will be some that rent more quickly for more, and others that rent more slowly for less. The biggest determining factor here is cleanliness.

Tenants like clean properties. The house or condo may be old and the neighborhood may not be terrific. But, if it's something they can afford *and if it's clean,* they may take it anyway.

A clean rental will be taken much faster and sometimes for more money than another rental comparable in every way except cleanliness. Therefore, as soon as we get the property, we need to be sure that it's clean.

Cleaning up means walls that are spotless, carpets that are free from dirt and major spots, and particularly bathrooms that have been thoroughly washed.

Whenever I rent out a property, unless the previous occupants left it spotless, which almost never is the case, I automatically have the carpets shampooed and the walls touched up with paint. (I even use the same paint, "antique white," in all the rooms in all properties so that I don't have to buy special paint and dirty areas can be touched up.) I have the kitchen and bathrooms carefully scrubbed and cleaned.

Quite frankly, it's not that expensive to do. And it makes the property shine for the prospective tenant. Typically, the cost of a thorough cleaning, including rug shampoo, will run under $500. The cost is more than made up for by swiftness in finding a tenant and often in better rent. Also, and perhaps more importantly, a tenant who wants to move into a very clean place is more likely to keep it clean.

External Appearance

When renting, some landlords worry a lot about external appearance. This isn't really necessary.

The location of the property speaks for itself, and there's nothing that can be done about it. The property is where it is, and we can't change its location.

Beyond location there's general neatness. A fresh coat of paint on the front will dress up even the dingiest rental. Being sure there is nothing lying around out front (like car parts from the previous tenant) and that the lawn (if any) is green and mowed also helps. So, too, does having a nice driveway. Nothing about a house looks worse than a driveway that is crumbling.

But these items are really minimally important to the prospective tenant. He or she isn't buying the place. The tenant usually doesn't really care what the neighbors think about the house. The tenant cares about the inside, where he or she is going to live. Therefore, extra money spent on fixing up the property externally is often wasted.

There is one exception, and that has to do with lawns and shrubs. We as owners want the vegetation around our property kept up. That way, when we need to rerent or sell, the place looks nice.

On the other hand, the last thing a tenant wants to worry about is watering someone else's property. Even if it's in the rental agreement that it's the tenant's responsibility to water, don't expect 99 percent of tenants to do it diligently. Therefore, money expended on an automatic (electric timer-controlled) watering system is usually money very well spent.

Raising Rents

Thus far, we have talked about getting the property rented the first time. Once we've rented it, however, our next goal will undoubtedly be to increase rents. This will give us additional cashflow and, in the case of apartments (and office buildings), increase the value of the property. (For large buildings, the value is directly dependent on the rental rate. We'll see how this works in detail in a later chapter.)

Raising rents is tricky. If we raise rents too far or too fast, our present tenants will move out. If we don't raise rents, however, we pass up a chance to increase our cashflow.

What's the Overall Rental Market Like?

Before even considering the raising of rents, we should make a revised analysis of the housing market. We should once again look up "For Rent" ads in the local paper, find those that approximate our property, and go see those rentals. Only in this way can we determine how competitive our unit is.

This is important, because our current tenants are going to do it as soon as we raise the rent.

Most tenants tend to stay where they are as a matter of inertia. The thought of moving is usually overwhelming. So rather than think about it, the tenants just keep paying the rent—until we change the circumstances. Increasing rents has a shock value. It reminds tenants of their true relationship with the landlord—strictly business. It also reminds tenants that they were looking for a place to rent when they found our place, so maybe they'll just continue looking.

You can be sure that as soon as you raise rents, your tenants are going to be out there, scanning the paper and looking at other rentals. That's why you need to do it first.

You need to know that when your tenants go out and look, they won't find that they can rent something much better for much less than they are paying you. If they discover that they can, they'll overcome their inertia and move. Only if they discover that they've got a pretty good thing going where they are will they stay.

How High Should Rents Be Raised?

Again, it's a matter of market conditions. We should survey the market, and if we discover that our rates are unusually low, we should feel justified in raising them. However, when we raise rents, we should understand that our tenants are immediately going to go out to see what others are charging. If they find our rental rate is comparable (and they can afford it), they'll undoubtedly stay. On the other hand, if they find our new rent is much higher than other rates, they'll move.

An interesting point here is that we can raise our rate a little bit higher than market and usually still keep our present tenants. Again, the reason is inertia. Let's say we are renting our unit for $1000 a month and we raise the rent to $1025. Now our tenant goes out to see what's available and discovers that a similar unit is renting for around $1000. Does this mean our tenant will automatically move?

Not necessarily. There's the effort and expense of moving. Maybe the convenience of staying is worth that extra $25 a month. For many tenants it is.

On the other hand, is getting an extra $25 a month, or $300 a year, worth it to us to risk losing a tenant? Most experienced landlords would say no. Let well enough alone.

For that reason, many landlords don't raise rents while they have a tenant in the property. They only raise rents after the tenant moves out.

How Often Can Rents Be Raised?

Never raising rents for fear of losing a tenant is a way of denying ourselves the rewards of owning property. What good is a rental if we can't charge top dollar for it? Why bother to be in the rental business at all, if that's the way we're going to play the game? (In the past it could be argued that the property was a great tax shelter. But as we've seen, that argument is strictly passé.)

Raising rents after a tenant moves out is easy. Most landlords try to bump up the rent 5 percent to see if the market will bear it. If it won't, they'll drop the rent back down to where it was before.

Raising rents for a current tenant is much more difficult. As we've just noted, the danger is that the tenant may move out. Yet, we really need to take the risk in order to get the best usage from our property.

A few years ago when inflation was soaring, raising rent every 6 months or, in some cases, every 3 months, was a common practice by some landlords. And they got away with it. They explained to their tenants that the price of everything was going up. Hence, they just had to raise rents.

Recently, however, inflation has been relatively low. Using the inflation argument usually won't work, particularly if the rental market around us hasn't gone up. As a result, rent increases have tended to be far less frequent.

Today, most landlords look for a rent increase of 5 percent annually. Often, it's on the anniversary of the month the tenant moved in. Of course, depending on market conditions, you may want to ask much less, perhaps 2 percent (or much more). You may also want to forego any rent increase for several years if the market you are in is particularly bad.

How to Tell Tenants Their Rents Are Increased

Tenants expect rent increases. They understand that it's one of the penalties they pay for renting and not buying. While they may not like it, they usually accept it as inevitable.

Nevertheless, the way tenants are told about a rent increase can make the difference between having them move out or stay. There is a whole psychology and a right way and a wrong way to communicate a rent increase.

Some landlords personally go around to each tenant and explain that the rent is going up. They then listen carefully to what each tenant has to say. They may even ask if there are any extenuating circumstances that would prevent the tenant from being able to pay the rent.

These landlords, though well-intentioned and often highly moral people, are also suckers. Any tenant, including you or me, who senses that the landlord is hesitant about raising rents is going to come up with reasons why the rent should stay the same. The reasons can be anything from the federal budget deficit to sister Jane's new baby.

The point is that no one wants to pay more rent, just as no one wants to pay more for a steak in the butcher shop. If we suspect the butcher is hesitant about raising prices for fear he or she might lose our business, we'll argue for a lower price. If the tenant feels the same way, he or she will come up with arguments why the rent should not be raised. That's why I feel that, whenever rents are raised, it should be done in a businesslike fashion.

The proper way is in the form of a business letter/notice written on formal stationary with our logo on top. Here are the typical contents of such a letter:

> Dear Tenant:
> As of the first of next month, the rent on your unit will be (*new rent goes here*).
> The reason for the increase is (*state any increases in expenses you may have had*) as well as the need to maintain a competitive return on investment.
> Your continued tenancy is valued. Should you have any questions or concerns regarding your rent, please feel free to call me.

There are several advantages to using a letter such as this. First, tenants have an opportunity to experience the initial shock of a rent increase in private. To put it another way, they don't have to react immediately to us.

Second, it gives them time to think. They can go look at competitive rentals. They can consider our reasons for raising the rent. They can see how they feel about staying where they are.

Third, we've left the door open for them to contact us. There could be a compelling reason, such as illness or loss of employment, why they can't afford a rent increase. In that case, they can come to us and explain the problem, and we may very well wish to forego the rent increase, temporarily.

Finally, but most important, the letter doesn't sound tentative. It states an already accomplished fact. The rent *has already been raised.* The raise will take effect the next month. This tells the tenant that we have already made the decision. We are not thinking about raising rents or wondering what they think about raising rents or maybe feeling like we ought to raise rents. We've already done it.

They can still present reasons why they should be an exception. But they don't have the option of discussing the decision to raise rents.

Note: It's important to understand that in most jurisdictions you *must give proper notice before raising rents.* In a month-to-month tenancy, that notice is typically 30 days. If you have a lease, you probably can't raise rents until the lease expires.

Concessions

Sometimes a rent increase requires us to make concessions. Let's say a tenant has lived in the property for a year without complaining about anything. We raise the rent, and suddenly the tenant has all sorts of complaints. The washers in the faucets leak, the carpet is torn, the screens need replacing.

This is one of the perils of raising rent. The tenant may get angry but, instead of moving, may decide to stay and punish us.

If, in fact, the complaints are legitimate, then as landlords we really do need to handle them—or risk losing a tenant. On the other hand, if they are petty and unrealistic, it's time to have a heart-to-heart talk with the tenant. We may need to make an appointment, stop by, and tell the tenant in no uncertain terms that, while we'll fix anything that's really wrong, we're not going to fix fantasy problems.

But be careful. A tenant who tries to punish you for raising the rents is probably unpredictable. He or she may suddenly decide to stop paying altogether or to do damage to the property. Here, again, you have to use common sense and not just a small bit of understanding human nature.

The Landlord Who Wants Only the Top Dollar

Occasionally, some landlords try to take common sense and human nature out of renting real estate. They go for one thing only—the top rental dollar. This takes the form of always charging the highest possible rents, always insisting on big rent increases, and never paying any attention to their tenants' problems.

This sort of behavior in a landlord tends to be self-defeating. Usually this landlord has longer vacancies, more property damage, and greater rent delinquencies than others. The reason is simple: Tenants are people, too, and they expect to be treated as such.

One of the most successful landlords I know is an older couple who own dozens of rental houses. They have some tenants who have been with them for more than a decade. They never get complaints from their tenants, unless a water heater leaks or something major goes wrong. They never have to worry about late rental payments and they never have long periods of vacancy.

Their secret? They act decently to their tenants. In exchange for tenant loyalty, they have fewer and lower rent increases. The tenants understand and respect this.

Their rental rate is never the highest (but it's not the lowest either), and they make sure that their properties are always clean and neat.

They take care of their real estate. And in their maturity, it has taken care of them, providing a strong income on which they live.

The Landlord Who Is Talked into Keeping Lower Rates by the Tenant

Finally, there is the landlord who, with all good intentions, tries to rent at the market rate (or tries to raise rents) but is intimidated by the tenant. As a result, he or she ends up either:

1. Renting for a lower rate

2. Not getting rental increases

3. Renting to an undesirable tenant

Some tenants are psychologically very powerful. They evaluate you as a landlord from the first meeting, trying to find weaknesses. If you're unsure about what you're doing, about your rights as a landlord, they can exploit you. Suddenly, they come up with legal-sounding reasons why you can't raise rents or why you are violating the intent if not the letter of the law by asking your current rental rate. This type of tenant may want you to install air conditioning and may hint at serious consequences if you don't. He or she may want a week's grace period in paying the rent.

The kind of tenant of which I'm speaking is a conniver. He or she is a person who knows how to get under your skin.

Experienced landlords recognize this personality at once. However, even novice landlords can identify the tenant. As soon as you in any way feel threatened by a tenant for no reason that you can identify, you can be pretty sure you are being psychologically manipulated.

The answer is simple: Don't rent to this sort of person to begin with. If they are already a tenant, be short and be firm with them. A 3-day eviction notice (common in California and other states to begin an unlawful detainer action) for rent even 1 day overdue has a sobering effect. So has a 30-day notice to quit if the tenant gives you a hard time.

Remember, it's your property, your money, and your peace of mind. Unless all three are satisfied, you won't be happy.

The Bottom Line

You want to get the highest rent you can reasonably expect from your property. You want to raise rents justified by market conditions. You're entitled to them, and they are the only way you are going to avoid a negative cashflow and show a profit on your real estate.

9

Eleven Methods of Changing Negative Cashflow to Positive

Our strategies thus far in this book have been aimed at the investor who intends to purchase real estate and what to look out for under the new tax law.

However, there are a great many of us who *already own property* who are even more concerned. This is particularly the case when the property we own is producing negative cashflow. In the past, we were able to write off this negative. Now our ability to do so may be eliminated or severely curtailed. What do owners with negative-cashflow properties do?

This chapter is aimed at current investors who have such property. Its goal is to provide realistic options for solving the problem.

1. Take Over Management of Property

If you are using a property manager, the first thing to consider doing is taking back the reins of control over your property.

Just doing this might turn your negative cashflow around. For example, if you're paying a property manager $75 a month, when you take over management, that $75 monthly expense suddenly stops. This alone may make the difference between negative and positive cashflow.

Secondly, there's the matter of repairs and maintenance. With a property manager, almost certainly these were hired out and chances are the rates were fairly high. In the past, I've used property managers, and I've found that the fees they charged for maintenance tended to be very high. In one case when a light switch went bad, the property manager sent out an electrician. Cost of the switch—$.99. Cost of the electrician—$65.

Or when the stove had a problem, a plumber was sent. Parts to clean a burner—$.35 worth of detergent. Labor—$55.

The property manager had an excellent explanation. "I can't have just anybody working on the electrical. What if the house were to burn down because of something they did? I can't have just anybody working on the stove. Again, what if something were to happen?" The argument was one of liability.

If you do the maintenance yourself, the liability argument remains. If you work on the electrical or gas system of a house and something goes wrong and the house catches fire, for example, and tenants are hurt, you can be held liable.

Nevertheless, in my own houses, I don't hesitate to clean the stove or to replace a light switch. I feel I'm competent to do those things. (You may not be. I'm not recommending you do anything that you aren't competent to handle.)

The point is that, when you do it yourself, you save money. A lot of money. One property manager I had charged me $100 to have the screens cleaned on a house. The screens cleaned? I later did that myself in half an hour with a hose!

It's not that I'm down on property managers. I'm not. In fact, they are the only way to go, if you can afford them. But if your property is producing negative cashflow, you need to look quickly at areas where you can turn it around. Taking over the management yourself is one of the fastest.

Remote Properties

A big problem with taking over the management of property is that frequently it's some distance away. If you're in California and your rental units are in Phoenix, you're hard-pressed to remove your property manager. After all, you can't be Johnny on the spot to show the property. And if the tenant has a problem, you can't economically hop on a plane to fix it. What do you do if you have property that's some distance away?

The answer here is simple. You don't buy property that is more than

30 miles away from home. If you currently do have property that's some distance away, sell it. Distant property with a negative cashflow is hopeless. There's no way to turn it around. Dump it.

2. Dump the Loser

As we've seen, property that is far away and that has negative cashflow, in my opinion, should be sold. But what about properties that are close to home? Is there a time when they should be sold as well?

Yes. But it's important first to identify those properties that are hopeless losers and should be dumped. With those far away, it's easy. With those close by, it can be harder.

That's not to say that a nearby property with a significant negative cashflow is hard to identify. If we have a condo on which we are losing $300 a month when it's fully rented and has no maintenance, we have a loser. In the old days, that loss might have been easily written off against our taxes. But today, we may not be able to do that. In this case, identifying the property to sell isn't hard. Sell the one with the big cash loss.

But some nearby properties are marginal. They seem to have great potential. Yet for one reason or another, they just never turn around.

One investor had a property that was this way. When it was rented, it showed a positive cashflow. But, for some reason, it was difficult to keep rented. Most tenants only stayed a few months.

It took the owner a relatively short time to rerent, usually two or three weeks. But she was losing those 2 or 3 weeks worth of rent three or four times a year. That was equivalent to having the place vacant almost a full two months annually. The result was that, on an annual basis, the property showed a huge negative cashflow, although on a month-to-month basis when rented, it had a positive cashflow.

The owner tried everything. She insisted on leases from tenants. In those cases, the tenants, after a few months, broke the leases.

What was the problem? It could have been bad neighbors. It could have been something intrinsically wrong with the design of the house. It could simply have been bad luck.

It really didn't matter what the problem was. Just the fact that there was a problem with the property was enough. In the old days, the negative cashflow could be absorbed by the tax shelter aspect. But with tax reform, the owner found that impossible. There was only one solution for her. Dump the property. That's what she did.

Today, investors simply don't have time to try to turn a problem property around. The negative on almost any property comes up too fast. As soon as we identify a loser, we should dump it.

Selling at a Loss

The problem with selling, of course, is that frequently the house or condo that's the loser is the one that is most difficult to sell. It may be in a depressed area or have features that detract from it's value. When we try to sell, we may find that we can only do so if we take a loss. Should we sell at a loss just to dump the loser?

That depends on several factors, which include:

- How much is our negative?

- How much would we lose in a sale?

- Can we economically and psychologically take losing money each month if we hold onto it?

The first two calculations are relatively simple. To arrive at net cash out, we just contact brokers in the area to find out what the property would sell for and subtract the costs of sale. Subtact that from our investment, and we find out how much, if anything, we lose.

Next we calculate the negative cashflow for the next 3 years on the property. Then we compare the figures.

If we would lose less by selling than by holding for 3 years, I would opt for selling. The property is a dog and we're better off without it.

On the other hand, if we lose more by selling than we would by holding for 3 years, we may want to reconsider. After 3 years, chances are we'll be able to increase rents. And if expenses stay constant, we could be working toward positive cashflow. Additionally, we may be able to sell for more after 3 years (though not necessarily).

Finally, there's the matter of the economic and psychological drain of losing money each month. Can we handle this? If not, then we should sell regardless of the loss.

Dumping a loser is not a good way to handle real estate. It means admitting we made a mistake. It often means taking a loss. But it may be better to admit the mistake and take the loss than to continue on hopelessly with negative cashflow.

3. Get a Positive Property to Offset a Negative One

Under the Tax Reform Act, all real estate is passive. (If you don't know what is meant by passive, reread the section defining it in Chapter 2.) That means that we can't write off real estate against our regular income.

It also means, however, that we can write off real estate losses against real estate gains. This provides an opportunity for some investors.

If we have a property that has a negative cashflow, one way of offsetting it is to buy another property with a positive cashflow. The negative can be used to offset the positive so that we achieve at least a break-even.

This is a simple answer that is, however, not quite so simple as it seems. To begin with, we don't want this solution to supercede the "dump the loser" solution previously noted. In my opinion, if we have a loser, we dump it. Don't try to offset the loss with a winning property.

On the other hand, if we have a property that has a small negative cashflow, say $100 a month. And we feel that the property will eventually turn around, then we may very well want to try to offset the loss with another property.

Quite frankly, it's not that difficult to find a property with a $100-a-month positive cashflow. Consequently, the prospects for offsetting a loser with a winner are fairly good.

When to Offset a Loser with a Winner

What this recommendation involves is putting good money in after good. If you already have a property, then chances are you put in some of your cash to get it. It may be a good property with good appreciation potential. Perhaps you counted on the tax savings to handle any negative. It's not your fault that the people in Washington changed the rules in the middle of the game. But that also doesn't mean that you now have to lose.

In such a case, investing more money to buy a positive-cashflow property can make excellent sense. All that you are doing is protecting your investment.

4. Trade the Property

This is an alternative that few people consider. However, it makes excellent economic sense. There are at least three good reasons for trading:

1. When we sell, we get all the taxable gain hitting us. When we trade, however, it may be possible to defer any gain onto the next property. There are distinct tax advantages to trading over selling. (*Note:* there are very specific rules and requirements for trading real estate. Be sure to check with a specialist in the field *before beginning* any trade.)

2. Often, we can trade a property to avoid selling at a loss. For example, let's say that we own a home that is losing $400 a month. We want to dump this loser in the worst possible way. However, if we sell, by the time we pay closing costs and lower our price sufficiently to find a buyer, we may take a beating.

On the other hand, we offer to trade. We find someone who has a small lot somewhere with just about the same equity as we have in the house. This person is looking for a house in which to live. We trade them the house. We get the lot. We get full price; they get full price. (One of the nice things about a trade is that the price stops being such a stumbling block. Traders are more concerned about equities.)

Since the lot is paid off, we don't have any negative (except for taxes, which are probably small). Since the person with whom we traded is going to use the house as a personal residence, he or she isn't concerned about the negative cashflow. Like the rest of us, they figure they are just going to be making monthly payments on the mortgage.

Eventually, if the lot isn't out in the desert or under water, it will probably be worth something. Consequently, instead of taking an immediate loss, we've projected our investment into the future in such a way that there's no negative cashflow. We've, in effect, buried our investment. We'll forget about it for a while and, eventually, it may grow into something quite valuable.

Of course, trades made in heaven like this don't happen all the time. We may need a three-way trade to get what we want. We may end up with another property that's only a little bit better than the one we originally had and need to trade again.

The point, however, is that we won't know what we can trade for, until we try. Trading should seriously be considered a realistic option.

How to Trade

If you haven't traded before, you'll certainly want to have the services of a trading broker the first time. There are very few brokers who regularly trade properties. Of all agents, 99 percent simply handle sales. You'll want to ask several brokers for recommendations before you find a trader in your area.

Traders belong to trading clubs. They usually meet weekly and, at that time, describe their listings and write up tentative deals. Deals written on your property are really just offers to trade. When you list your property with a trading broker, you may find you have all kinds of crazy offers coming in (and some not so crazy, too). People may want to trade for boats, cars, diamond rings, or anything else. You may find that trading definitely expands your options.

I have found that trying to trade for out-of-area properties is more difficult. If you're in Kansas and you want to trade for a property in Minneapolis, you may find it tough going. But, it's not impossible. Sometimes interstate trades do work out. Although trading should not be considered your first option, it definitely is an option worth considering.

5. Take in a Partner Who Has Shelter Opportunities

Yet another alternative is to consider selling a portion of your negative cashflow property. Perhaps you don't want the negative because, under the new tax law, you can't write it off. However, there are people who are still able to write off real estate losses against other income. (Remember the $25,000 allowance noted in Chapter 1?) Becoming partners with one of these people can turn a property around.

How to Do It

The idea is that the partner buys some of your equity and pays a portion of the expenses. In exchange, the partner gets all the tax write-off. You get some of your cash out and stop having to worry about the negative cashflow. Both of you divide the profits when the property is sold. In a case such as this, because the partner may have more to offer than you do, you might well have to give him or her a bonus in the form of increased equity, but it should work out in the long run.

The real trick, of course, is finding the right partner. That should start becoming increasingly easy as the effects of the new tax law begin taking hold. Increasingly, owners of negative-cashflow properties will be looking for such partners. And increasingly, people who have the possibility of retaining a real estate write-off will become aware of the benefits they can offer and the opportunities that are available to them.

Initially, however, it's going to be pretty much a word-of-mouth thing. You'll want to keep in contact with a good many brokers, spreading the word around about what you need. You'll also want to contact accountants and financial planners, those who help investors with their taxes. They, too, may provide leads.

Note: It's important to understand that even when you find the right partner, you still have to set up a partnership arrangement that the IRS will accept. Therefore, you should consult a competent CPA, tax attorney, or other tax planner.

6. Refinance

This is so simple a solution that sometimes we forget about it. It may be possible to refinance the debt on our property, thereby achieving smaller payments and eliminating negative cashflow. It certainly pays to check this out. Generally speaking, refinancing will lower our payments if:

1. We get a longer-term loan.
2. We get a reduced interest rate.
3. We combine several small loans.

Let's take these one at a time. First, a long-term loan makes sense *if* we already have a short-term loan *or* if we have held the property for a number of years. For example, by going from a 15-year (short-term) to a 30-year mortgage, we cut our payments by 15 percent. That's usually the difference between negative and positive cashflow. Or, if we have held our property for, let's say, 10 years, we may have paid a significant portion of our original loan balance. Now when we refinance, even for the same interest rate, we will achieve a lower monthly payment.

Second, refinancing at a lower interest rate will reduce our monthly payment. However, the rate usually would have to be decreased by a minimum of 3 percent for it to make any difference.

Finally, we can combine several small loans. Second and additional mortgages are typically for a shorter term (often 3 to 15 years) and at a higher interest rate than we could get on a new first mortgage. By getting a new 30-year first mortgage for the full amount of the other mortgages on the property, we may be able to significantly cut our payments.

Refinancing may be a quick and painless way to get rid of negative cashflow. But it does have a down side of which we should be aware. Refinancing is expensive.

Today, to refinance a first mortgage usually costs between 4 and 5 percent of the mortgage value. And that assumes there are no special costs, such as termite damage repair or other work on the property. If we borrow $100,000, we are talking about paying $4000 to $5000 additional just for the refinancing. Of course, these costs usually are just tacked onto the mortgage amount. (This assumes we have sufficient equity in the property. Normally a new first that's refinanced can't be for more than 80 percent of the appraised value.)

Nevertheless, the costs of refinancing reduce our equity. When it finally comes time to sell, we will get our profit out of the property *less the costs of obtaining the refinance* (assuming the costs were added to the mortgage). Therefore, I always suggest carefully evaluating goals for the property. If we're planning to resell within the next 3 years, it may not pay to refinance even to get rid of a negative cashflow. The costs of the refinancing would simply be too heavy. On the other hand, if we plan to keep the property long-term, then refinancing may definitely be the way to go.

7. Renegotiate the Current Loan

Again, this is a potential solution that most investors never consider. Most of us are simply convinced that once we take out a mortgage from a lender, negotiations are finished. A more realistic tack to take, however, is that negotiations never end.

A friend bought a condo for rental purposes a few years ago in a growing area. However, shortly afterward, oil prices started to fall and oil companies, which were the hub around which the area was growing, closed down.

Almost overnight the area took on a depressed pallor. People moved away. Businesses closed and it became difficult to rent the property. Eventually, my friend found that in order to keep his property rented, he had to cut rents to the point at which he had a $300 negative on the property.

Before the Tax Reform Act, he hadn't been in such terrible shape. He was able to deduct the losses from regular income. But after the Act, in his case, no deduction was possible. It was a straight out-of-pocket, $300-a-month loss.

He wanted to dump the property. However, try as he might, he could not sell or trade. The area was so depressed that no one wanted to take on his loser.

Finally, in desperation, he went to the lender, which was a savings and loan association. After half an hour of talking, he got past the floor personnel and was ushered into a back room, where the vice president in charge of real estate lending had an office. She was not happy to see him.

My friend explained his predicament. He was losing money on the property. Yes, he could keep it rented. But no, he could not do so at break-even. Unless he got some relief somewhere, he was going to have to let the property go into foreclosure.

The loan officer did not like to hear that. The S & L already had thousands of REO properties taken back because, in the slumping economy, the owners could not make payments. The S & L's very solvency was being threatened.

Rather than take back another property, the loan officer suggested a compromise. The lender would restructure the mortgage and offer a lower interest rate and a longer term. The interest rate was substantially below market.

As a result, my friend suddenly found that he could rent the property at break-even, which he is currently doing. His hope is that eventually, when the local economy turns around, as he's sure it will, he will be able to sell at a profit.

Not all lenders will be willing to renegotiate. But these days, with parts of the economy in steep recession or even depression, some certainly are. You'll never know until you ask.

8. Give the Property Back

In number 7, the suggestion was to renegotiate the loan with the lender, and the assumption was that the lender was an institution, such as a savings and loan.

But what if the lender was the seller? Many times property is purchased through seller financing. What if the house or condo you want to dump fits this bill?

My suggestion is that you go to see the former owner and explain the situation exactly as it is. You may, for example, have a $300 negative cashflow on the property. You cannot tolerate that. You explain the situation to the seller and offer to give the property back *if* the seller will return at least a portion of your down payment.

You can expect the former owner to laugh at this suggestion, *until* you point out that if he or she does not agree to this, you will simply stop making payments on the mortgage. You will continue to collect rents for the 4 to 7 months it takes for the former owner to foreclose on the mortgage he or she gave you. The former owner will have the hassle, the time spent, not to mention the money out of pocket required to foreclose on the property—UNLESS he or she agrees to take it back and make some concessions.

At the very least, you may get the former owner to renegotiate the loan. Or he or she may be willing to take the property back and give you some financial consideration. Either way, for a real dog that's breaking your back, this is a viable alternative that definitely should be considered.

Deed in Lieu of Foreclosure

On the other hand, your lender may indeed be an institution, such as an S & L, which refuses to renegotiate the mortgage. What can you do then?

If you are so desperate as to be willing to give up your equity, you can offer to give the lender a deed to the property in lieu of foreclosure. The S & L will save costs, and you won't have on your record the credit stain of a foreclosure. For some investors this may be the final solution. If you don't have much cash invested in the property, it may not be such a terrible one at that.

Note: Giving a deed in lieu of foreclosure probably won't affect your credit rating in terms of getting bank loans or credit cards. But it will affect your ability to get new mortgages. Almost all lenders these days ask the following question on a mortgage application:

"Have you ever given a deed in lieu of foreclosure?"

If you answer yes, you stand an excellent chance of having your mortgage application turned down. (Including a letter explaining extenuating circumstances may prove helpful.)

Lying about giving a deed in lieu of foreclosure by answering no, when you have indeed given such a deed, is not recommended. In many cases, if the lender discovers the lie, which it very well may, it could be cause for refusing to give you the mortgage, for rescinding the mortgage if it was already given, or for suing for damages.

9. Use a Lease Option

This is another way of removing negative cashflow from your property, but it has certain limitations that are important to understand.

A *lease option* is giving the tenant the option of buying the property. Typically, the lease option calls for the tenant to lease the property for 2 to 3 years. During that time, a certain portion of each monthly payment is applied toward the down payment. At the end of the option period, *the tenant* can choose either to buy the property or not. Let's take an example.

I have a house on which I am losing $200 monthly. I am already at my maximum rental rate. So I now find a tenant who is willing to give me a lease option. I rent the property to the tenant for $200 a month more than my previous rental rate. Now I have achieved break-even, no negative.

Why is this tenant willing to pay a higher rental rate? The reason is that, out of each monthly payment, I will credit $300 towards the down payment. After 2 years, when the lease option is up, the tenant will have a credit of $7200. If the full down payment required to refinance is, for example, $15,000, the tenant need only come up with $7800 more plus closing costs.

Advantages

The advantages to me are twofold: First, I have the property rented long-term for enough money to break even. I've eliminated my negative cash-flow. Second, I have at least a tentative sale. At the end of 2 years, the tenant, hopefully, will buy the property at a price we've agreed upon.

The advantages for the tenant are also twofold: First, he or she has locked in a price on a property 2 years in the future. Second, part of each month's rent is going toward the down payment.

Disadvantages

The disadvantage to the tenant, however, are also twofold: First, under a lease option, the tenant is normally expected not only to pay the rent, but also to handle all the upkeep that normally would fall to an owner. This is an additional expense.

Second, the tenant is paying a higher-than-normal rent. There's nothing wrong with this, as long as the tenant follows through and makes the purchase, since a large portion of the monthly payment is going toward the down. But, if the tenant does not or cannot fulfill the purchase, than paying the higher rent is going to waste.

The disadvantages to the landlord are threefold: First, if the tenant decides to purchase, I've given up part of my equity each month in order to achieve break-even. At purchase time, I have to give the tenant a credit of $7200 (per the example). I have, in effect, traded equity for cashflow.

Second, I've locked in a sales price 2 years ahead based on today's market. If the property goes up in value, I don't benefit; the tenant/buyer does. (Some lease options are written so that the sales price will be determined by independent appraisal at the time of purchase. This benefits the seller, but it's hard to find a tenant/buyer who will go along with it.)

Third, in *most* cases, the tenant never exercises the option, never buys the property. In *most* cases the tenant either cannot qualify for a new loan or cannot come up with the additional cash required for a down payment and closing costs.

Thus, to some extent, a lease option is a kind of pipe dream for both tenant and landlord. The tenant thinks he or she is going to buy. The landlord thinks he or she has got a sale. But 2 (or 3) years down the road, both suddenly discover that things just aren't working out as everyone thought they would.

Of course, this isn't always so terrible for the landlord. He or she has the property back after having received at least break-even for several years. It's probably better than just renting it out. Unless, about half-way through the lease option, the tenant realizes it isn't going to work out, stops taking care of the property and, in worst case, stops paying the rent. Then the landlord has a real hassle.

Fortunately, this worst-case scenario rarely happens. More often than not, after a year or so, if the tenant realizes that things are not going to work out, he or she will ask to be released from the lease. Most land-lords, to avoid any possibility of damage to the property and nonpay-ment of rent, will agree.

A lease option, therefore, is a sometimes successful way out of nega-tive cashflow. Yes, it can provide an excellent escape hatch when it works. Even when it doesn't, however, for the landlord it often provides a year or more of trouble-free, break-even cashflow.

10. Improve the Property to Increase Rents

Sometimes the reason a property will not produce the desired rent can be identified. Perhaps it's a matter of the carpeting. Our condo has old, stained, and torn carpeting. We can only get tenants by offering a lower rent. And the tenants we get tend to be the kind that don't take care of the place.

Or maybe we have a two-bedroom house and we are in a rental mar-ket where everyone has children and is looking for at least a three-bed-room house.

Or perhaps the property has large back and front yards which are weed-strewn. Prospective tenants take a look at the yards and decide they don't want the place.

Sometimes with a rental there is a definable feature that is causing us to receive a reduced rent. The carpeting or the number of bedrooms or the yard is holding the property back. If only the problem were correct-ed, we could get enough rent to at least break even.

If the property has the potential to break even and it doesn't cost too much for the improvement, my suggestion is to do the work. For exam-ple, new carpeting can be put into a rental for $12 a yard. Good-quality carpeting, as of this writing, can be obtained for $20 a yard. A 1500-square-foot rental typically requires 130 yards to completely carpet (kitchen, baths, and closets frequently are left uncarpeted). That's a minimum expenditure of $1560. It might be worthwhile in order to get a break-even rent.

Similarly, a garage might be relatively inexpensively converted to an extra bedroom. If it can be done for a few thousand dollars, it too might be worthwhile in order to boost rents.

A sprinkler system and basic landscaping might cost a thousand dollars. It might be very well worth the money to get the higher rent.

The point is simple: Sometimes it pays to improve the property to get rid of a negative cashflow.

When It Doesn't Pay

A word of caution. Just improving the property may not necessarily guarantee increased rents. It probably will when there's a definable problem. But, if the lower rent or the tenant problems are caused by other factors, such as poor location or the age of the house, then no improvements may help.

It's important to carefully evaluate the property before spending money. Calling in a broker or a property manager as a consultant to get ideas may help. The rule is, improving properties with definable problems can improve cashflow. Improving properties where the problem is due to unalterable conditions is like throwing good money after bad.

11. Sell the Property to a Corporation

This is a very limited solution for those who own corporations. What we are speaking of are wholly owned corporations that some people have for their business. For example, some investors have a corporation that handles their funds. Doctors, attorneys, writers, and other professionals may also incorporate.

It may be possible to sell the property to the corporation. Then, any tax loss is a corporate loss. Presumably any corporate loss can be offset by any corporate income. Thus, the property could still, in effect, be used as a tax shelter.

The problem here is that the rules for incorporating, including reporting requirements, are strict, and just maintaining a corporation can be fairly expensive. Consequently, you wouldn't want to form a corporation just for the purpose of handling a rental house. (Besides, you would then need to put your own income into the corporation and once you did that, how would you effectively and easily get it out?)

However, if you already have an existing corporation, this might be a feasible answer. As of this writing, the consequences of doing this have not yet been approved by the IRS or tested in court. Hence, it remains a risky alternative.

These then are eleven possible solutions to negative cashflow. If you already own property and are worried because of the way the government has changed rules in midstream, consider using one or more of them. They may be just what it takes to turn your property around.

10
Profits in Apartment Buildings

Some of the greatest opportunities in real estate may be occurring in the apartment building market over the next few years. In large part, these will be caused by the Tax Reform Act. Those who are in a position to take advantage of them should be able to reap substantial rewards.

Understanding the Potential

As noted in Chapter 1 of this book, the rationale behind the coming boom in apartments is based on three premises:

1. The new tax law will cause owners who purchased apartment buildings largely for the tax shelter advantages they previously offered, to dump those properties. This should cause an increasing number of apartment buildings to come onto the market, thus causing downward price pressure.

2. Lower interest rates have allowed many tenants to step up into ownership by buying their own homes. This has resulted in a short-term dwindling of the overall tenant pool. As landlords fight over a smaller tenant base, rents will necessarily come down, and this, in turn, should also put downward pressure on apartment building prices.

3. Because much of the tax shelter advantage of apartment buildings has been eliminated by the new tax law, new construction has almost

ground to a halt. This will be scarcely felt in the short run. But over the next few years, it should create a significant and dramatic shortage of rentals (particularly if we have higher interest rates, which would slow the number of tenants who become owners, as in item 2).

The net result of these factors is an immediate surplus of rental units and a corresponding lowering of apartment building prices. This may be followed in a few years by a dramatic increase in apartment building values as rental rates go up.

Seeing the Opportunity

Thus, an opportunity may be presenting itself for those who are in a position to take advantage of it. Namely, those who buy apartment buildings when they are depressed in price and have the wherewithal to hang onto them for several years could reap enormous benefits when the market turns around. It's the old story of buy low and sell high, with the usual risks. But at least at this juncture, the coming turns in the market seem to be more exaggerated and clearer than usual.

While those who are familiar with apartment building investment should immediately see the argument, those who are new to the field may be wondering about a couple of points. For example, how does increased rent result in higher apartment building prices? Or why should new construction be virtually halted because the tax shelter advantages have been cut? Or why are old owners dumping their apartment buildings in the first place?

In this chapter, we'll look at the answer to these and other questions and in so doing clarify the real opportunity that may exist in this field.

How the Price of an Apartment Building Is Determined

Like the price of a jar of mayonnaise or a book or anything else, ultimately, the price of an apartment building is determined by supply and demand. The price is what a buyer is willing to pay.

But in apartment buildings, determining what a buyer is willing to pay has been refined. As experienced investors know, the price of an apartment building is ultimately determined by its rental income.

We calculate how much income will be generated from rents each year, then subtract our expenses to find out how much the building nets. If the apartment building *nets* $7000 a year, and we want to get 7 percent on our money, then we know we can afford to invest $100,000. (This is called *capitalizing the net income* and is often used in appraisal.)

However, determining the true *net* income can be tricky. There are many variables, such as increases in taxes, vacancies, or repairs, which could eat into the net rental income.

In addition, rarely do investors in real estate pay cash. Financing is common practice. As a result, depending on the quality of the mortgage (interest rate and term) our *net* can be higher or lower.

Thus, rather than use net, common practice has dictated that the gross income of the apartment building be used roughly to determine price. While net may be difficult to accurately determine, gross is much easier. It's simply the total of all rent monies collected over a year *before* any expenses, such as taxes, mortgage payment, repairs, insurance, and so on.

Price Based on Gross Rental Income

It's necessary to remember that out of gross income must be paid all the normal expenses of ownership; consequently, gross income on apartment buildings does not really compare with, for example, true yield on bonds, for which there are no expenses. Gross income is simply an arbitrary figure commonly used in determining price.

Here's an example: At a given time in a given market, investors might agree that a 10 percent gross rental income is appropriate for apartment buildings. Thus, if a building's rental income were $100,000, then $100,000 should represent 10 percent, or ⅒, of the price. To determine the price, we simply multiply the rental income by 10 to get a figure of $1,000,000.

On the other hand, if the *same* apartment building were bringing in $50,000 annually in gross rents, then we should be prepared to spend $500,000 for it (10 times $50,000 equals a price of $500,000).

The point is that the price varies depending on the gross rental income. The greater the gross rental income, the greater the price. The lower the gross rental income, the lower the price.

Gross Income Multiplier

It has become common practice to use a shorthand method of calculating price based on the gross annual income. It is called the *gross income multiplier,* or GM. It only requires that we know two items: the gross income (before taxes, mortgage payment, insurance, and other expenses) from the apartment building and the multiplier that is currently being used.

Let's say we have an apartment building that is producing $35,000 a year in gross income. From talking with brokers, other investors, and sellers, we know that the GM for that area, type, and age of apartment building is currently 8. What is the correct price? The following illustrates *how to use the GM to determine price:*

Gross income	$ 35,000
Multiplier	×8
Price	$280,000

Is it really that simple?

Quite often, yes. I've seen small apartment buildings bought and sold with no more calculations than were just illustrated.

That's unfortunate, because a lot of other factors enter into the picture, such as the amount of expenses (determined by the condition of the building and the quality of tenants) as well as the quality of financing (the prevailing interest rates, the term, and so forth). Nevertheless, in the trade, the GM is usually the first calculation made and often the most important.

Applying the GM

The purpose of bringing up the GM is not to explain appraisal, but rather to explain the relationship between rents and price and, indirectly, how the coming rental boom could force prices of apartment buildings through the roof. The GM clearly shows why apartment prices could go up significantly in the future if rental rates increase.

Let's suppose the GM is 6 (which historically would be rather low). We have an apartment building of four units, each of which is rented for $350 a month. We bought the building a year ago at what we considered a bargain-basement price of $100,800, based on the GM of 6. The following illustrates the *use of the GM in determining purchase price:*

Monthly rent per unit	$350
Number of units	×4
Total monthly income	$1400
Annualized	×12

Gross annual income	$ 16,800
Multiplier	×6
Purchase price	$100,800

Now, however, the shortage of rental space has finally hit. Tenants are calling us to see if we have any rentals available!

Because of the increased demand, we raise rents, moderately at first, to $375 a month. When we multiply that by 4 units times 12 months times a multiplier of 6, we suddenly discover that raising our rents by just $25 a month has increased the price of our building by $7200, to $108,000.

Six months later we jump rents another $25 a month, up to $400, and discover that the value of the building has gone up to $115,200, or an increase of another $7200. In fact, each time we increase our rents, the value of our property increases. Here is a chart showing the increase in value at various rental rates for this building.

Increase in Price Caused by Increase in Rents

Rent per unit	Monthly income	Annual income	Multiplier	Price
$350	$1400	$16,800	6	$100,800
375	1500	18,000	6	108,000
400	1600	19,200	6	115,200
425	1700	20,400	6	122,400
450	1800	21,600	6	129,600
475	1900	22,800	6	136,800
500	2000	24,000	6	144,000
550	2100	25,200	6	151,200
575	2200	26,400	6	158,400
600	2300	27,600	6	165,600
625	2400	28,800	6	172,800
650	2500	30,000	6	180,000
675	2600	31,200	6	187,200
700	2700	32,400	6	194,400

What should be evident is that even small increases in rental income have great impact on price. Raising rents directly and significantly increases the value of our building. This is quite different from a rental house, the price of which is determined by the price of comparable homes in the area (normally determined by buyers, most of whom intend to live in rather than rent out the property). In an apartment building, price is determined almost solely based on rent. Raise the rent of a rental house and, normally, you don't increase the price. But raise rents in an apartment building and you have dramatically raised the price. In the example, for every dollar increase per unit per month, the value of the building goes up in value by $288!

Thus, if we can indeed buy when rents are low and then subsequently raise rents as the coming rental shortage may allow us to do, we can translate real estate economics into palpable profits.

Increasing the Multiplier

The gross income multiplier is usually most fascinating to those new to income property. (Experienced investors know the problems of it, some of which will be explained later in this chapter.) What's even more fascinating, however, is that the multiplier rarely stays constant. That is, it moves up or down, depending upon enthusiasm in the marketplace for this type of investment.

Back in the 1950s and 1960s, multipliers of 4 and 5 were common. During the skyrocketing real estate market of the late 1970s, multipliers of 12 to 14 were used in some very hot areas. Most recently, multipliers of between 8 and 9 have been more common.

If we buy property during an apartment building recession, we can expect to purchase during a time of very low multipliers. If, however, a rental shortage subsequently makes owning apartment buildings highly desirable, the multiplier might increase. And an increase of the multiplier results in large and immediate increases in the value of our property.

Effects of Increasing the Multiplier

Gross income	Multiplier	Price
$30,000	6	$180,000
30,000	7	210,000
30,000	8	240,000
30,000	9	270,000
30,000	10	300,000
30,000	11	330,000
30,000	12	360,000

Notice that increasing the multiplier increases the value of the property *without any increase in rents!*

Historically, multipliers go up and down, depending on market conditions and investor demand. If we can buy a property when the multiplier is low and hold it until the multiplier goes up, we can make significant profits without even having to raise rents.

Pitfalls of the Multiplier

Income multipliers allow us quickly to translate any rental increase into increased property value. However, multipliers work against us when rents go down. Remember, one of our original premises was that, as tenants convert to owners during a period of reduced interest rates, rental rates will fall.

If we buy an apartment building when the rental rates are still declining, we could easily see our building value drop significantly. In fact, it goes down just as fast as it goes up. In the example, we saw that for each dollar the rental income per unit increases, the value of the building goes up by $288. However, the converse is also true. For each dollar the rental income per unit *drops*, the value of the building goes *down* by $288.

Thus, it would behoove us to be very careful either to buy at the bottom or to be sure that we can weather any economic storm caused by falling rental rates.

Additionally, just as income multipliers themselves can go up, so too can they decline. If we buy with a multiplier of 9 only to find that later the multiplier has gone to 6, we will discover that our building has lost a third of its value.

Considering True Return

But the biggest pitfall of the gross income multiplier is that it doesn't take into account the true return on a building. For example, let's say that we have $100,000 to invest. That may buy us a $500,000 apartment building. The gross rents from the building are $62,500 a year. That's a GM of 8 which, we are told by numerous brokers in the area, is appropriate.

Gross rents	$ 62,500
Multiplier	×8
Price	$500,000

Everything seems to check out okay. However, when we calculate our expenses, including taxes, insurance, mortgage payment, management, and repairs, we find that they run $70,000 a year. Thus, our apartment building has a negative cashflow of $7500, as follows:

Gross rents	$62,500
Total expenses	−70,000
Cash loss	$ (7,500)

Those new to the field might laugh at such a deal, spending $100,000 in cash to purchase an apartment building that then loses $7500 in cash per year.

However, it has been far more the rule than the exception. Investors bought because of the tax advantages of owning the building. What was lost in cash through simple economics often was more than made up for in tax savings. For example, on the above building, depreciation might be $20,000 annually. When depreciation is added, the total annual loss comes to $27,500.

The following illustrates the calculation of the *tax advantage of owning a negative cashflow apartment building prior to 1987*:

Annual cash loss	$ 7,500
Depreciation	+20,000
Total loss	$27,500
Tax bracket	×50%
Tax savings	$13,750
Cash loss	−7,500
Annual profit	$ 6,250

Thus, though an investor might indeed have lost $7500 out of pocket *before* taxes, he or she might have shown a $6250 profit *after* taxes, or a profit of a little better than 6 percent. The tax advantages of real estate made it all work out in the end.

Problems with the GM Today

Using the GM to calculate the price on apartment buildings, which has commonly been done, worked in the recent past primarily because of tax advantages. Even if the building came out in the red, with a buyer in the right tax bracket, it would all work out.

Today, of course, that is all turned around. The tax advantages have largely been removed, and the building with the loss remains the building with the loss, even after taxes.

As a result, two things are likely to happen. Either the GM used to calculate the value of apartment buildings will have to fall significantly to make up for the loss of tax advantages *or* a new method of calculating price will have to be used.

My own feeling is that both are likely to occur. In the future, we are probably going to see far more realistic GMs used. We may find that GMs in the 4 to 7 range are common, which are significantly lower than those used in the past.

In addition, we are going to see investors begin to use new kinds of procedures (such as the internal rate of return) for evaluating the price of a building.

A New Way to Look at Apartment Buildings

In the remainder of this chapter, we are going to look at a new method for evaluating an apartment building for use after the Tax Reform Act of 1986. This method will be familiar to experienced investors but may be new to those just entering the field. If you use it, you shouldn't go too far wrong.

As noted in Chapter 1, my feeling is that apartment buildings of four units or less are best for small investors. The reason, as also noted, has to do with rent control. You are far less likely to be bothered with rent control in small units and can thus be free to raise (or lower) rents to match market conditions.

How to Evaluate an Apartment Building

Let's say we've found a small, four-unit apartment building. We figure we can get a $200,000 mortgage after we invest $50,000 of our own money. We plan to offer $250,000. But, is it a good deal?

To begin with, we have to define what is and is not a good deal. If we assume that rental rates are going to go down in the immediate future and then rise in the more distant future, an appropriate strategy might be to buy at the bottom and hold for at least 5 years, then hope to sell for a big profit.

The profit we anticipate comes at the time of sale. Therefore, during those 5 years, we do not need to be overly concerned about a return on our investment. What we do need to be concerned about is that we don't have any negative cashflow during those years. (If you aren't sure why this is bad, reread the earlier chapters.)

Therefore, our goal with this building is to buy and then at least break even. If we can break even, we'll assume we've got a good deal. If we have negative cashflow, then we'll have to assume the deal is bad.

(As noted earlier, there are other strategies. For example, we could be aiming to hold for rental income. If that were the case, we would need to have less of the purchase price financed. We would need either to buy a less expensive building with our $50,000—perhaps one for $100,000—or come up with more money.)

Determining Break-Even: Income

Determining break-even is a function of comparing rental income with expenses. The four-unit building is currently rented for $500 per unit. What is the gross annual rental income?

Obviously, four units times $500 is $2000, times 12 months is $24,000 a year rental income. That, however, is only the most optimistic assessment of rental income. There are bound to be vacancies.

Many investors use a fixed figure of 5 percent for vacancies. My own experience suggests that this is not a good thing for a small investor to do. If you own several hundred units, taking an average figure of 5 percent may indeed work out. But, if you own only one building, it is far better to try to get actual vacancy figures.

Assuming the building is several years old, ask to see the rental receipts book the owner kept. For tax purposes, if no other reason, every owner keeps a book detailing all rental receipts. If you are a legitimate buyer, the owner should not hesitate to show it to you. (If the owner won't show it to you, don't buy the building—the chances are too high that something is really amiss.)

The book should list the names of tenants and the amounts and the dates each paid, hopefully going back several years. You should, either yourself or with the aid of a bookkeeper, go back a couple of years and look for three things:

1. Find out how much total rental income was taken in *each month* and the average for the last two years. This should quickly paint a picture of the vacancy rate. If there are four units rented for $500 apiece, but the rental receipt book shows an average income of $1750 a month, you know that, on the average, one unit is vacant for two weeks out of each month. That's a vacancy factor of 12½ percent, quite high for most areas. (To find the vacancy factor, just divide the anticipated monthly or annual rental income into the actual received rental income—in this case $2000 into $1750. This gives you the occupancy rate. The corollary is the vacancy rate.)

2. In addition, check to see how many names appear in the receipt book. Ideally with four units, there should be only four names, indicating no movement of tenants at all (i.e., the same four tenants have been there for the whole time). Realistically, however, tenants move rather frequently. For most apartment buildings, typical periods of occupancy are about 9 months. In a four-unit building, this means that, over the course of a year, there should be between six and eight different tenants.

If there are a great many different tenants over a year, it means that the building has a high turnover rate. This is a yellow flag. Even if the actual rental income is close to anticipated, having a high turnover means that there are going to be added expenses with regard to cleaning up after each tenant. Also, you have to ask yourself why the tenants move out so often. Is there a problem the landlord hasn't disclosed?

3. Finally, write down the names of the current tenants and, if possible, the names of the past tenants. The purpose here is to confirm the rents. With the owner's permission (why, after all, should he or she object), contact each current tenant. Explain that you are planning to purchase the building and are wondering if there are any problems. Along the way, ask to confirm the rental rate shown in the receipt book.

(Some prospective buyers shy away from actually contacting the tenants. This is a bad idea. You're going to have to talk with them after you buy the place, so better to meet them beforehand and see what you're up against.)

As for former tenants, what I like to do is to prepare a letter that looks something like this and send it to them (after first telling the owner of my intent):

> Dear Former Tenant:
> I am in the process of purchasing the apartment building located at 23 Elm Street. The rental records indicate that you were a tenant from June 1 to Sept. 30 of last year and that your rental rate was $500 a month.
> Could you please confirm this in the place provided below and then return this letter in the enclosed envelope?
> Sincerely,
>
> _____
>
> Dates of tenancy: From: To:
> Rental rate:
> Comments:

This simple letter can be very revealing. Just send it to the tenant's name *in care of the apartment building*. Tenants almost always file a change of address form, which the post office honors for 1 year. Thus, the letter will be forwarded to them. Most will be happy to respond.

Why Such Curiosity Over Rents?

I'm sure that many readers new to investing are curious as to why I've gone to such lengths to determine the actual rent received. Why contact present and former tenants? Why not simply believe the rent receipt book of the owner?

The answer is that, while I'm a firm believer in the goodness of humanity, I don't let this belief blind me to the fact that some people will resort to many kinds of deceit to promote their own self-advantage. I have seen apartment buildings where the owner blatantly falsified the rental receipt books. I've seen buildings where the landlord moved in relatives at no rent (but who were willing to say they were paying full rent) in order to give the appearance of full occupancy.

Remember, the price is largely determined by the rental rate. Thus, increasing that rate (by obscuring vacancies or lower rents) can make a big difference. You'll recall in our initial example that an increase in rent of only $1 per month per unit increased the value of that building by $288. The incentives to play around with the rental figures are too strong to let us simply hope for the best and trust to the honesty of the owner.

Of course, we've just been discussing the determination of the true rental rate for an existing resale. For new buildings, a different procedure is required. It is outlined in detail in Chapter 5. The rules that are given there for determining true rents in single-family homes also apply to apartment buildings.

Determining True Expenses

Once we've found the true rents, our next task is to get as accurate a picture of expenses as possible. Some expenses are quite easy to determine.

Easy Expenses To Determine

Mortgage Payment.   For an existing mortgage, check the mortgage payment book or contact the lender. For a new mortgage, the lender will give you the exact figure.

Taxes.   These are a matter of public record. However, be aware that in some states (such as California) the taxes levied depend on sales price. If the original owner paid $100,000, the taxes may be based on that amount.

If you're paying $200,000, the taxes may be doubled once you gain ownership! Be sure to check with a competent broker or accountant for the laws in your state.

Insurance.   Again, easily found out from your insurance broker. But be sure to include the cost of liability as well as fire insurance.

More Difficult Expenses to Determine

Some expenses are more difficult to determine and may require some careful research:

Repairs.   Just as with rental receipts, ask to see the current owner's ledger for past repair costs. Here, however, with a small apartment building, the owner may simply say, "I don't keep such a ledger. I just pay the bills and keep the receipts for tax purposes."

That may be the case. Or the owner may not want you to know just how many repair expenses there really have been.

My suggestion is that, if you're not very familiar with the construction of buildings, hire a building inspector to evaluate the property. (Building inspectors should be licensed contractors. They often advertise in the yellow pages of the phone book.) Typically, the cost is only a few hundred dollars. They should give you a written estimate of the electrical, plumbing, and heating systems, as well as an evaluation of the structure, foundation, roof, exterior, and other features of the building.

Use this information to help determine what you are likely to pay for maintenance each month and what repairs may be necessary over the next few years. (A new roof, for example, can cost many thousands of dollars. You need to know if the present one is adequate when you make your initial evaluation of the deal.)

Try to handle repairs by averaging. Check such things as putting on a roof, buying a new water heater, or painting. If any of these are likely to occur during the 5 years you plan to own the property, find out how much each will cost and set up a reserve to cover it.

For example, your inspector tells you that the water heater is bad and will need to be replaced soon. A new water heater for the apartment building costs $500. You plan to keep the building for 5 years; that's $100 dollars a year, or $8.33 a month. When you calculate your expenses, include that $8.33 and put the money in a separate account. If you don't, you'll suddenly come up against a big unexpected expense sometime after you purchase the property.

Similarly, reserve accounts should be set up for other anticipated expenses, such as a new pool pump or new roof. The reserves simply are a good way of helping average out the cost over a number of years and being aware of true monthly expenses.

Regular Maintenance.   In addition to special repair reserves, there is also monthly maintenance. This can be something simple, such as a pool service or gardener. Or it can be a bit more complicated, such as cleaning an apartment after a tenant leaves.

Don't be the kind of foolish landlord who thinks that the previous tenants are going to leave the property in tip-top shape. Even if the tenants were angels, once they move their furniture out, you'll be able to see scratches in the wall paint and discoloration in the carpets and even a few broken tiles or pieces of flooring. This has nothing to do with negligence or lack of upkeep. It's just the sort of thing that comes from living in a place over time and from moving in and moving out. (Most people are very surprised to see how "damaged" their own homes look, once they move out.)

This means that you can regularly expect to paint, clean, or recarpet and otherwise fix up an apartment *each time* a tenant moves out. Do not expect the tenant to cover this cost in his or her security deposit, because it does not fall under the heading of damage. Rather, it's simply normal wear and tear.

It will take some experimenting to figure out exactly how much to allot here. However, if you do the work yourself, it's usually just the cost of a gallon or two of paint, some carpet cleaner (and the rental of carpet cleaning equipment), and some elbow grease. If there is no real damage, $50 will usually cover it.

On the other hand, if you hire it all out, the cost can be $500 or more each time a tenant moves out.

Don't overlook this cost. It's real. It's something you'll have to pay. And you should include it when you initially calculate the expenses of running the apartment building.

Management.   Most people who manage their own apartment buildings don't take out a management cost. They just figure that it's time they'll spend on the property.

I find no fault with this as long as you do, in fact, have the time to spend. If you're retired or if your business activity allows you the time to tinker with the property, fine. However, if you will need to take time away from your regular work (for which your employer will dock you or which will cause you to lose business), then by all means you *must* set aside a management cost.

In any event, it's going to cost something to advertise for rerenting. In addition, some owners set aside a reserve for legal costs in case of a possible eviction.

Finding Out if the Property Is Break-Even

Finally, after we've done our homework, we can put it all together and come up with the bottom-line results: Does the building at the very least break even? Here's a typical example:

Apartment Building Evaluation

	Monthly	Annual	
Income			
Gross rental income	$3000	$36,000	
Real vacancies	−400	−4,800	
Net rental income	2600	$31,200	$31,200
Expenses			
Mortgage	$1000	$20,000	
Taxes	300	3,600	
Insurance	60	720	
Repair (reserves)	150	1,800	
Maintenance	+350	+4,200	
Total Expenses	$2560	$30,320	−30,320
Positive cashflow			$880

It turns out that this property does indeed at least break even. (It has a tiny positive cashflow.) Evaluating it on the basis of its adequacy in terms of the new tax laws makes it a good prospect.

Down Payment, Financing, and Price

Our evaluation assumed a $200,000 mortgage and a $50,000 down payment.

Price	$250,000
Down	−50,000
Loan	$200,000 (10% for 30 years)

However, we did not use the traditional method of a GM to determine price. Unfortunately, the owner did. She took the gross annual income and used a multiplier of 10 (which she had been told was common for the area), arriving at an asking price of $312,000. That's what she figured the building was worth, according to the traditional methods of evaluation. However, the two methods of evaluation resulted in a significant difference.

Owner's method	$312,000
Our method	−250,000
Difference	$ 62,000

Were we willing to pay the owner's asking price, we would have two choices: (1) to increase the mortgage amount significantly, turning the property into a negative cashflow investment (an additional $62,000 of mortgage would cost about $550 a month or more, assuming 10 percent for 30 years) or (2) we would have to pay that $62,000 as additional cash down payment.

Whose Method of Evaluation Is Correct?

Who's right, us or the owner?

Before the 1986 Tax Reform Act was signed, the owner's case was stronger. Any actual cash losses, when added to depreciation, could be written off against ordinary income. A taxpayer in the 50 percent bracket might very well be able to pay the owner's price and still break even, after taxes.

Today, however, that's almost an impossibility. Today, the buyer's (our) case is stronger.

Increasing the mortgage in order to be able to pay the extra $62,000, thereby turning the property into a negative cashflow investment, makes little sense. As we've seen in earlier chapters, negative cashflow is to be avoided, if at all possible.

On the other hand, increasing the down payment makes even less sense (unless we want to hold for income). In the example shown, we are already committing to a $50,000 down payment on a property with an annual return of only $880 (our positive cashflow). If, alternatively, we were to invest that $50,000 in the bank at 7 percent, our return would be $3500. That means we are actually losing $2620 annually (before compounding).

Savings account	$3500
Property	−880
Lost interest	$2620

Of course, it could be argued that we are willing to absorb the $2600 a year in lost interest (about $13,000 over 5 years) in the hope of making a lot more money when we eventually sell the property.

However, as we invest more of our cash into the property, that hoped-for return down the road seems slimmer and slimmer. Consider: If we had invested $112,000 (about what it would take to give the owner her price) in a 7 percent savings account, our annual interest would be $7840. This means that by investing in the property, we have an annual loss of interest of about $7000. Over 5 years, that would be $35,000. Suddenly the idea of putting the money in a no-hassle savings account becomes far more appealing.

The New Pricing Structure

The point here is to show that a new pricing perspective is going to be necessary for evaluating apartment buildings. Owners are going to have to accept lower GMs or face the prospect of not selling their properties. (In this case, a GM of 8 would be quite respectable.)

As of this writing, this has indeed happened. In many areas of the country, GMs of 8 are appearing. In some areas, GMs of 7 and even 6 are becoming prevalent. (Of course, should interest rates increase, thus increasing the expenses on the property, it may be necessary for owners to adjust their expectations even further downward.)

All of this points to the possibility of obtaining property at reduced prices in the very near future.

The Goal

Our goal, as noted earlier, is to hold the property until the coming rental shortage forces prices up. When that happens, we will be able to ask a higher price for the property we bought. For example, let's say that after 5 years, rents went up by $200 a month. Assuming the same vacancy factor, our rental income would go from $31,200 to $40,800, and the value of the property *at the same GM of 8* would soar to $326,400, for a profit of $76,400. The following illustrate the *effect of rent increases on potential sales price:*

Income	$ 3,800
Vacancy cost	−400
	$ 3,400
Annualized	×12
	$ 40,800
Multiplier	×8
Sales price	$326,400

And therein lies the whole point of the deal: to hold, break even, and then either keep the eventual new positive cashflow or sell for a profit.

Why Not Count the Potential Rental Increases Immediately

I have heard some advisors point out that, because we can expect rents to rise perhaps in the next 2 or 3 years, we can afford to take some cash loss in the first years. For example, if rents rise $200 a month after 2½ years, in theory we can still break even *over 5 years* if we have a negative cashflow of $200 the first 2½ years. The positive cashflow from the end of the ownership term overcomes the negative cashflow from the beginning of the ownership term.

The problem is that we can't predict the future. What if rents don't rise? What if they fall further before plateauing or turning around?

When we aim for break-even at the onset, we go for safety. When we accept any negative at all, we are walking dangerously out on a limb.

Aiming for break-even will not, of course, guarantee a safe deal. But it is undoubtedly a safer deal than one with negative cashflow.

If you want to take advantage of the predicted boom in small apartment buildings, I encourage you to seek out no-negative cashflow properties (or positive cashflow properties). To my thinking, they offer the greatest potential combined with the most safety.

11

A New Direction for Limited Partnerships

For limited partnerships, this is the worst of times and the best of times.

Today, limited partnerships offer some of the best opportunities in real estate. Through this vehicle, a number of small investors can pool their resources and establish a strong equity position in a property that none of them individually could afford. They can get positive cashflow plus appreciation. For low-leveraged, high-return investments, limited partnerships may currently, in fact, be the ideal vehicle.

Unfortunately, the flip side is that many partnerships that were in effect prior to the new tax law are suffering greatly. These are partnerships that were formed, in large part, to take advantage of real estate tax shelters. Suddenly, one of the major reasons for their very existence has been eliminated.

Because partnerships have been both good and bad for the investor, there is a lot of confusion about them in the area of real estate. The result is that many investors are steering clear of *all* partnerships until the air clears, and the area of partnerships is suffering.

Quick-Change Artists

To understand the problems and benefits of partnerships more clearly, let's begin with existing real estate partnerships. During the end of 1986 and the beginning of 1987, shortly after the new tax law was passed, partnerships produced some rather unusual twists.

It seems that I'm regularly besieged by partnerships wanting me to participate. Prior to the passage of the tax reform bill, I received mail describing the wonderful tax savings that many of these partnerships offered. Buy into this one or that one and receive a big write-off immediately plus additional write-offs over the next 4 or 5 years.

Then the tax bill passed and almost immediately the tone and substance of the offerings changed. Almost overnight, instead of a tax shelter, I was being offered high annual returns on my money. At a time when bank interest rates were sometimes below 5 percent, I had partnerships offering me 12, 16, even 18 percent return on my money.

What was most interesting was that, in some cases, the partnerships offering the highest returns were, in fact, the very same partnerships that only a month earlier had offered no-cash returns, touting tax shelters instead! How quickly the leopard changes spots.

The Truth About Existing Partnerships

I'm sure that I'm not the only one to receive such literature and I'm equally sure that many would-be investors have wondered about this. Can a partnership that is set up as a tax shelter switch in midstream to one that suddenly makes big profits?

Yes, and no.

Until late 1986, virtually all limited partnerships were indeed put together to emphasize the tax advantages of owning real estate. They accomplished this primarily through heavy (and sometimes over-) leveraging.

For example, let's say the ABC company is a small limited partnership of twenty-five individuals. (Small limited partnerships operating within the boundaries of a state often need not register with the SEC but are subject to state law. We'll have more to say about this in a few pages.) The partnership's goal was to invest in small industrial buildings.

Each partner put up $10,000. They did this by borrowing the money. Thus, they put up no cash out of pocket and, under then-current tax rules, were able to write off the interest on this loan.

The partnership's initial capital was $250,000. The general partner (GP) took $50,000 as an up-front fee for efforts in putting the partnership together. (This up-front fee is often one of the drawbacks of small limited partnerships.) The group then invested in a building worth $2,000,000. The following illustrates the *financial structure of the deal* for the industrial building:

Purchase price	$2,000,000
Loan	−1,900,000
Down payment	100,000
Starting capital	$200,000
Down payment	−100,000
Remaining capital	$ 100,000

Because there was so little down and because the loan was such a high percentage of the purchase price (95 percent), the rental income from the property produced a negative cashflow. Thus, the property lost $20,000 a year in cash. This was paid by the GP out of the remaining capital so that the partnership did not have to come up with any additional cash.

The $20,000 annual cash loss plus depreciation on the big building, however, was passed through the partnership directly to the partners. The total annual loss was $100,000 (with depreciation). Each partner, therefore, got a tax write-off of $4000.

$$\frac{\$100,000 \text{ annual write-off}}{25 \text{ partners}}$$
$$= \$4000 \text{ individual write-off} \times 50\% \text{tax bracket}$$
$$= \$2000 \text{ individual tax savings}$$

Thus, an individual in a high tax bracket, by borrowing the money to join the partnership, could invest no cash, write off the interest on the money borrowed to get into the partnership, and, as a return, get an annual tax write-off of $2000 in cash.

While not all partnerships were structured exactly like this, many, in fact, were. Most often the participants were those in high tax brackets who could take advantage of the partnership's tax shelter aspects.

Changes Caused by the New Tax Law

After the tax bill of 1986 was passed, the ABC partnership suddenly found itself in deep trouble. The partners could no longer write off the interest on the $10,000 they borrowed to get into the partnership.

What was worse, because they were in high tax brackets, they could no longer write off the $4000 annual loss that passed through to them. They had no tax savings and no interest deduction. The investment suddenly had turned worthless.

What was even worse, they still owed the original $10,000 plus interest that they had borrowed.

Needless to say, the partners set up a loud hoot and holler, and the

GP was hard-pressed to do something about the partnership deal. But what could he do?

Altering Existing Partnerships

The GP looked at the industrial building's finances. It had gone up in value about $50,000 since the ABC partnership had purchased it. But the loan balance was almost the same. (There is very little payback in the first years of most loans.) The facts were these:

Value	$2,050,000
Loan	−1,900,000
Equity	$ 150,000

If the loan had a high interest rate, refinancing to a lower rate would help by reducing monthly payments and thus cutting expenses. But the loan originally had a low rate and it was for the maximum 30-year term. After a careful examination, the GP determined that, for the present, there was no way to reduce expenses (or raise income) on the building. That left the partnership two choices:

1. Hold the property until things got better.
2. Sell immediately.

The GP (who in a limited partnership usually makes the decisions in such matters) decided that he didn't want to listen to the cries of the limited partners, so he decided to sell.

It took a while, but eventually a buyer was found who was willing to pay $2,050,000. However, the broker who procured the buyer took a 6 percent commission, or $123,000. And there were more than $20,000 in closing costs.

Sales price	$2,050,000
Commission and closing costs	−150,000
Gross to partners	$1,900,000
Mortgage	−1,900,000
Net to partners	$ 0

The GP got out of the industrial building, but at a total loss of capital. However, the partnership still had $80,000 of its original capital left. With this, the GP went looking for a new building and found one, for a price of $240,000. The new deal looked like this:

Price	$240,000
Down payment	−80,000
Loan	$160,000

On this property, the partnership put up fully one-third of the price in cash. Because there was such low leveraging, the building was able to show a $12,500-a-year net cash profit. This the GP dispersed to the limited partners, resulting in each of them receiving $500 a year.

They stopped complaining. It wasn't great. But it was better than it had been. The $500 helped pay the interest on the $10,000 they had originally borrowed. And, as the GP pointed out, if they kept the building, eventually rents (and their cash return) would probably grow. Hoped-for appreciation could eventually make back all the capital lost in the previous industrial building deal.

Thus, ABC partnership was able to revise its tax shelter goal to a positive cashflow goal. Unfortunately, in the process it lost most of its capital.

This, in general, is what many existing partnerships have attempted to do. Either by selling or trading current properties and then buying new properties into which they were lightly financed, they have tried to turn negative cashflow into positive.

Many have succeeded. Unfortunately, others have not. In the latter case, the ultimate result may be the collapse of the partnership and foreclosure on the building (which could result in a significant tax liability for the limited partners).

The Difference with New Partnerships

Having thus seen some of the problems of existing partnerships, we have also touched upon the promise that new partnerships offer. By pooling resources, partners can secure large equity positions in property and thus get strong positive cashflow.

As another example, let's say DEF partnership was formed *after* the 1986 tax law. It had essentially the same structure as ABC partnership: twenty-five individuals who each put up $10,000. After the GP took out his share, the partnership had $200,000 to invest.

Three Differences

There were some important differences, however:

1. Instead of borrowing the original $10,000, most of the partners took it out of savings. They realized that the interest on most consumer borrowing (home mortgages are an exception) was no longer deductible.

2. Additionally, instead of being high rollers in the 50 percent tax bracket, most of the new partners were small investors. The amount they invested in the partnership was a substantial portion of their life savings.

3. Most important, the GP looked for a large equity position in a small building.

The Property

The GP found a small apartment building which cost $300,000. The partnership put up two-thirds of the price in cash. The mortgage therefore, was only $100,000.

Price	$300,000
Down payment	−200,000
Mortgage	$100,000

Because of the low leveraging, the partnership was able to achieve a positive cashflow of $25,000 a year (the amount that income exceeded expenses). Thus, each partner received $1000 a year, or a 10 percent return on the investment. (At the time, banks were paying under 6 percent, so the partners felt this was a strong return.)

On top of this, the partnership hoped that rental rates would go up significantly over the next 5 years, allowing them eventually to sell the property for a strong profit. Thus, the partners got not only a good annual return but also the promise of equity appreciation down the road.

Why Buy into a New Partnership?

From the above examples, it should be clear that the partnerships that are usually best able to take advantage of the opportunities offered by the new tax law are newly formed. Older partnerships frequently are struggling to hang onto, sell, or trade heavily leveraged property they acquired under the old tax laws. Buying shares in an old partnership, therefore, can sometimes mean buying into someone else's headache.

In addition, the goals of partnerships today are significantly different from those prior to 1986. Today, the goals are to invest in *low-leveraged* properties. By putting in lots of cash, the partnerships hope to show a strong positive cashflow.

The positive cashflow is returned directly to the partners (return on investment). Additionally, the long-term goal is to sell for a substantial profit down the road. Thus, the partners look forward both to annual income as well as to long-term profit.

Small Versus Large Partnerships

When investing, we have a choice of going with a small, unregistered partnership (as were those in our examples) or with a large SEC-registered partnership. Many investors new to the field wonder about the pros and cons of each.

As noted earlier, small partnerships, depending on local state law, may not have to register as a security with the SEC. They often are found by contacting lawyers or accountants or other investors. As a result, they do not have the benefit of federal regulation. Although they are regulated to some degree by individual states, these small partnerships, nevertheless, tend to be far riskier ventures.

However, as a way for small investors to group together to buy a low-leveraged building that each partner could not afford individually, they are excellent vehicles. The key to success is *to know personally with whom you are investing*. If everyone in the partnership is on about the same level and you all have similar goals, then there is a true opportunity for success and profits.

As these small partnerships blossom and begin to take large equity positions in property, they will become highly desirable.

SEC-Registered Partnerships

On the other hand, the really popular partnerships as of this writing are the large, SEC-registered ones. These are partnerships which are, in almost every state, often sold by stockbrokers.

Large, SEC-registered partnerships often seek to raise millions, tens of millions of dollars. Then they invest that money, *sometimes without any financing or leveraging,* thus producing high returns for their investors. Recently, these partnerships have offered significantly higher returns than most other financial instruments. In addition, as we've already noted, they offer the potential of getting equity appreciation. Thus, they have become quite popular.

The drawback to these partnerships is that, like their smaller cousins, there is usually a heavy up-front load that reduces capital. Additionally, as the number of these types of equity partnerships increases, they will compete to produce ever higher rates of income, which could lead some to invest in riskier properties.

Just because the partnership is SEC-registered does not automatically mean it's safer. The safety often is more a factor of the prudence of the GP.

Problems and Pitfalls in Buying into Partnerships

Here are some general problems to understand and pitfalls to avoid when buying into partnerships.

Loss of Control in a Limited Partnership

There are two distinct classes of partners in a limited partnership: the general partner (GP) and the limited partner (LP). Each class of partner has different responsibilities and obligations.

The GP, for example, normally must be personally responsible for the venture and must manage and otherwise see it through.

The LP, on the other hand, has limited liability. If something goes wrong, it's not the LP's problem. In addition, by the terms of the partnership agreement (and in order to maintain it's IRS partnership tax status), the LP normally *may not in any way participate in the operation or management of the business.*

Some investors are thrilled at not having to manage or operate the partnership. However, others worry. Not being in charge means, to them, that they are at the mercy of the GP. If the GP turns out to be incompetent, negligent, or a downright crook, the LPs have relatively few options.

This is the reason that some investors opt for the big SEC-registered partnerships. They feel that, because the GP is a professional management organization, they are protected. Maybe. But I've seen incompetence in big organizations as well as small.

Incompatibility in General Partnerships

Of course, a limited partnership is not your only option. If you and several friends want to pool your resources and buy a property, then you can form a *general* partnership. You can all be active participants. The rules for forming such a partnership are normally far less rigorous than for limited partnerships.

A word of caution, however. If you form a general partnership, be sure that all the partners are compatible. Nothing could be worse than to raise money, invest in a property, and then find that one partner always wants to do things differently. Instead of calm decision-making sessions, you could end up with vicious arguments that make the whole project unpalatable. To get out of the bad situation, you and the other partners might end up selling at a loss.

In a general partnership situation, be sure you know with whom you are dealing. (My own experience has disabused me of ever wanting to be involved with a general partnership. Expectations are always different no matter how clearly things are spelled out. Some partners are always disappointed. To me, a general partnership is like a marriage with all the drawbacks and none of the advantages.)

Lack of Liquidity

This is usually a problem only with small partnerships. In a large partnership, if partners want to get out, the GP usually offers liquidity by agreeing to buy their interests.

In a small partnership of, for example, fewer than ten people, liquidity is a major consideration. Let's say that six of us decide to pool our resources and buy an apartment building. We are 6 months into the deal and Shelly, one of the limited partners, suddenly has a personal financial crisis. She needs her money out, immediately.

The trouble is that all of the money is already invested in the apartment building. The idea was to buy, get monthly income, and hold for 5 to 10 years. No provision was made to get the money out sooner than that. "But," Shelly explains, "I had no idea I'd have this emergency."

Now the partnership faces a crisis. On the one hand, it could probably ignore Shelly's demands, depending on how the documents were drawn up. On the other, the partners, being compassionate people, want to help her out. So they take out a second mortgage on the property to pay off Shelly. Unfortunately, this increases the leverage and significantly cuts into the positive cashflow.

The problem here is liquidity. In a small partnership, there is no good solution. Even if you as a partner are committed to leaving your money in the property for years, another partner could have trouble and need hers or his out sooner.

Documents

The only real protection that the limited partners have are the partnership documents. Unfortunately, there is no standard way these are written. They can be written carefully, so as to provide in some measure for problems such as liquidity, or they can be written carelessly, in which case a limited partner in trouble could force the dissolution of the partnership.

Typically, with large, SEC partnerships, the documents are written by experienced attorneys, and the rules and regulations are spelled out clearly and equitably. But with a small partnership, this is not always the case. Sometimes the partnership documents are drawn up by one of the partner's relatives who happens to be an attorney.

To protect yourself, it is vital, particularly in small partnerships, that you have a competent attorney draw up the agreements and documents. To be sure they are done right (assuming you don't yourself know), you need to have them reviewed by a person familiar with partnership agreements.

Getting a Competent GP

Anyone, virtually anyone, can be a GP. All that person has to do is form a partnership and get limited partners to contribute. Therefore, it behooves the limited partners to spend some time examining the credentials of the GP.

While there are many things to look for, the most important, in my opinion, is experience. Has the GP put together partnerships before? If so, how have they done? (Call former partners to find out.)

Is the GP experienced in the type of property he or she wants to buy? A GP with a strong track record in apartment buildings could fall flat trying to invest in commercial property. The two are not the same, and expertise in one does not automatically mean expertise in the other.

The Goal

As noted, partnerships in today's post–tax reform era require a different perspective. Instead of looking for properties that lose money, partnerships, just as individuals, need to seek out properties that have a positive cashflow.

Often, this is much easier for partnerships, which have more capital, than it is for individuals. Thus, we can expect many more partnerships to be formed in the coming years. In judging them, you won't go far wrong as long as they offer no negative cashflow.*

---

* To learn more about partnerships, I suggest my book, *Riches In Real Estate* (McGraw-Hill, 1981).

Appendix **A**

Property Evaluation Sheets

Property Evaluation Sheets

The goal of this book has been to describe the kind of property that will show a profit in the post–tax shelter era: basically a property which has no negative cashflow.

The idea is fairly simple and straightforward. However, finding suitable properties can be confusing and difficult. How are we to know *before we buy* that one property will produce a positive cashflow, while another will produce a negative one? Sellers and brokers will often point out only the positive aspects of the property and downplay the negatives. We may make judgments on the basis of incomplete or inaccurate information. As a result, our decisions could be faulty. In the worst case, we could buy thinking we'll end up with a property which has positive cashflow (or at the least will break even) only to discover that it actually costs us money out of pocket each month.

To help us ascertain the true income-producing ability of a property, the following charts have been created. They help analyze rental income and real estate expenses.

When you are looking to purchase your next investment property, consider using these sheets. They may help you avoid some real problems; they could aid you in finding a superior investment.

As you go through these sheets, watch out for any no answers. They could spell trouble.

Tenant Market Evaluation Sheet

	YES	NO
1. Is the surrounding tenant market "blue collar"?	___	___
2. Are there several large employers in the area (such as a factory, hospital, or public facility)?	___	___
3. If there is a single large employer, are its prospects good for continuing in business?	___	___
4. Are there other similar rentals nearby?	___	___
5. Are they charging comparable rents?	___	___
6. Is the vacancy factor below 5 percent?	___	___
7. Is the anticipated rent at or below competitive rental rates in the area?	___	___
8. Is there a local, widely read paper in which to advertise for tenants?	___	___
9. Are security deposits commonly collected in nearby rentals?	___	___
10. Is the past vacancy factor of this property low?	___	___

Apartment Building Evaluation Sheet

	YES	NO
1. Is the GM normal for the type, age, and area?	___	___
2. Will the owner provide you with a copy of the rental receipts book?	___	___
3. Do present tenants confirm the owner's statement of rents?	___	___
4. Do former tenants confirm rents and dates of occupancy?	___	___
5. Do you have an accurate statement of monthly mortgage expenses *prepared by the lender?*	___	___
6. Will taxes increase as a result of a change of ownership?	___	___
7. Has the building been evaluated by a professional inspector?	___	___
8. Have reserves been set aside to cover repairs?	___	___
9. Have *all* normal maintenance features (such as gardening, clean-up, and utilities) been added to expenses?	___	___

10. Has a reasonable charge been added for management? ____ ____

11. If you are planning to manage the property yourself, are you sure you won't be docked from your regular job or lose business income? ____ ____

12. Have you checked the income/expense sheet to be certain that the property will at least break even? ____ ____

13. Is this property *similar in every significant way* to other nearby properties, thus allowing your calculations to be comparable and accurate? ____ ____

14. Does each unit have its own utility meter? (If not, how is payment for utilities to be made?) ____ ____

15. Is the project currently non–rent controlled, and is it likely to stay that way? ____ ____

16. Has the owner disclosed and agreed to pass on to you any advance rent and security deposits collected? ____ ____

17. If the units are leased, do the leases have at least one year to run, or are they all expiring? ____ ____

Single-Family Home/Condo Evaluation

                                                                      YES   NO

1. Have you confirmed the present tenant's rental rate? ____ ____

2. If the property has never before been rented, have you conducted a rental survey of the area to find out rental rates of homes? ____ ____

3. Are there in the nearby vicinity the type of tenants you are seeking? ____ ____

4. Does the current tenant have sufficient income to continue meeting rent payments? ____ ____

5. If the property is leased, was the last month's rent plus a security deposit paid in advance? If it was, will the owner transfer it to you? ____ ____

6. Have you established a reasonable vacancy allowance and subtracted it from anticipated annual rental income? ____ ____

7. Has a competent person (professional inspector) viewed the property? Are there no significant repairs needed? ____ ____

8. Have you set aside a reserve for any needed repairs? ____ ____

9. Have you *accurately* determined what maintenance will cost? ____ ____

10. Do you have an accurate estimate of what it will cost to clean up and rerent after the current tenant moves out?

11. Are you getting the lowest interest rate and longest-term financing available?

12. Will the tenant pay all utilities? If you have to pay some (such as garbage collection and water), is there a maximum you will pay after which the tenant must pay?

13. Will the property taxes remain the same as a result of your purchase?

14. Is the property free from any significant detracting features (such as a broken slab, or landslide or flooding problem)?

15. Have you carefully estimated all repairs and determined real income? Does the property then at least break even?

Neighborhood Evaluation Sheet

YES   NO

For residential properties only:

1. Is this a neighborhood in which you would be willing to live or, at the least, collect rents?

2. Does the neighborhood pass the "graffiti test"? (No graffiti on any walls within three blocks in any direction.)

3. Does the neighborhood pass the "lawn test"? (No more than one unkempt lawn per block.)

4. Does the neighborhood pass the "broken car test"? (No broken cars being repaired or lying unattended within three blocks in any direction.)

5. Are the properties across the street and immediately on either side well kept?

6. Is the route between the property and major shopping and work areas free from traffic problems and/or does it have adequate public transportation?

7. Is the property in the direction of growth for the community?

8. Are there major industries, office buildings, commercial centers, or other sources of tenants nearby? Are these facilities well kept or do they detract from the neighborhood's appearance? ⎯⎯ ⎯⎯

9. Are there schools and shopping and recreational facilities nearby for the tenants? ⎯⎯ ⎯⎯

10. Is the ratio of rentals to owner-occupied dwellings low in the neighborhood? (The more rentals in the area, the greater the transient population and the greater the chances of properties being left unkempt.) ⎯⎯ ⎯⎯

Repair Evaluation Sheet

YES NO

1. Has the water heater been replaced within the past 3 years? (If not, it may have to be within the next 5.) ⎯⎯ ⎯⎯

2. Is the roof less than 20 years old, if shingle, or 10 years old, if composition? (An older roof may need repairs or replacement.) ⎯⎯ ⎯⎯

3. Is the carpeting free of permanent stains and does it still have loft? ⎯⎯ ⎯⎯

4. Are the appliances all working adequately? Is the dishwasher less than 3 years old. (If not, it may have to be within the next 3 years.) ⎯⎯ ⎯⎯

5. Has the air conditioner been reconditioned or replaced within the past 3 years? (If not, it may have to be within the next 5 years.) ⎯⎯ ⎯⎯

6. Are there screens and/or shutters on all windows? ⎯⎯ ⎯⎯

7. Are there screens on the doors? ⎯⎯ ⎯⎯

8. Have all the faucets been replaced within the last year? (If not, they may have to be within the next 2 years.) ⎯⎯ ⎯⎯

9. Has the property been free of any drain problems? ⎯⎯ ⎯⎯

10. Has the electrical system been inspected by a professional? Is the property free of any aluminum wiring or below-code wiring that may need to be replaced? ⎯⎯ ⎯⎯

11. Does the house have copper or PVC plumbing? (Galvanized steel corrodes within 20 years in some areas and may need to be replaced.) ⎯⎯ ⎯⎯

12. Are there door handles on all doors, do the door locks work adequately, and do the doors all close? ⎯⎯ ⎯⎯

13. Have the garage door springs been replaced within the past 5 years? (If not, they may have to be within the next 3 years.)

         _____   _____

14. Is the property free of holes, water marks, mold, or rot which will require immediate repair before the property can be occupied?

         _____   _____

Maintenance Evaluation Sheet

	YES	NO
1. Will tenants do minimum gardening work (or is a gardener required)?	_____	_____
2. Will tenants maintain pool (or is a pool service required)?	_____	_____
3. Can the property be rented without a pest control service? (If not, how often must it be used?)	_____	_____
4. Is the clean-up cost after a tenant leaves less than $250? (If not, is a reserve set aside for it?)	_____	_____
5. Are there cleaning people available in the area to handle the property's clean-up needs?	_____	_____
6. Will the property need to be completely repainted on the inside more often than every 3 years? On the outside more often than every 7 years?	_____	_____
7. Is the carpeting or flooring free of needing any special care?	_____	_____
8. Is the property free from any special maintenance requirements (such as for a jacuzzi tub, bird house, other feature)?	_____	_____

Property Management Evaluation Sheet

	YES	NO
If you manage the property yourself:		
1. Have you had experience in collecting rents, dealing with tenants, and handling other management duties?	_____	_____
2. Do you have an advisor in case there are unforeseen problems?	_____	_____
3. Do you have an attorney to handle evictions?	_____	_____
4. Do you have an adequate rental or lease agreement?	_____	_____

5. Do you have an ad and know where to place it to get tenants?

6. Do you have time to show property to prospective tenants?

7. Are you close enough to handle routine management chores?

8. Are you prepared for emergencies (e.g., when the tenant calls in the middle of the night to say the water heater has burst and is flooding the property)?

9. Are you set up to find gardeners, pool maintenance people, and repair personnel, and then disburse checks to them for work?

	YES	NO

If you hire a property management firm:

10. Will the firm handle *all* management, or are you required to participate?

11. Does the firm have a written property management agreement?

12. Does the firm meet guidelines for your "active participation" in running the property under the new tax law? (See chapter 1.)

13. Does the firm respond promptly to tenant requests and problems?

14. Does the firm screen prospective tenants?

15. Does the firm charge a normal and acceptable fee?

16. Does the firm charge a normal fee for routine maintenance and repair?

17. Does the firm respond promptly to your phone calls and letters?

18. Do you get written statements?

19. Are checks forwarded promptly?

20. Is the firm licensed?

Partnership Evaluation Sheet

	YES	NO

For limited partnerships:

1. Has the GP had at least 5 years experience in the specific type of property to be acquired?

2. Are the documents professionally and competently
prepared?   ____   ____

3. Is the partnership free from unwarranted and high
up-front fees?   ____   ____

4. Is the seller unaffiliated with the GP?   ____   ____

5. Is the partnership paying a commission of less than
10 percent for the realtor's buying the property?   ____   ____

6. Is the GP prohibited from asking for additional
funds? Are the limited partnerships nonassessable?   ____   ____

7. Does the GP have sufficient net worth to carry the
project if there are problems?   ____   ____

8. Are the fees to be charged for management no more
than 5 percent annually?   ____   ____

9. If the GP receives additional participation in profits, are they taken out after the limited partners have
first received their profits?   ____   ____

10. Is there a priority system for returning the limited
partner's capital before any money goes to the GP?   ____   ____

11. If the partnership is large, is it SEC approved? Is
there a load charged by the brokerage firm selling it
of less than 8 percent?   ____   ____

12. Is there a provision made for liquidating your por-
tion in case of emergency?   ____   ____

13. Can your money be invested for less than 7 years
before capital appreciation will occur? Will you receive an annual return on your investment? Will it
be at least equal to the current T-bill rate?   ____   ____

14. Are the goals of the partnership, i.e., the specific
property to be acquired, spelled out (or is it a blind
pool)?   ____   ____

Income/Expense Evaluation Sheet

Calculations should be done on an annual basis. The results can be di-
vided by 12 to arrive at monthly figures.

INCOME
    Total rents $_____
    Less vacancies   −_____
    Net rent $_____ $_____

EXPENSES
      Mortgage $_____
      Taxes   _____
      Insurance   _____
      Repairs   _____
      Maintenance _____
      Management   _____
      Reserves   +_____
      Total expenses $_____   – _____

POSITIVE/NEGATIVE CASHFLOW $_____

Index